Places for Learning, Places for Joy

Places for Learning
Places for Joy

Speculations on
American School Reform

THEODORE R. SIZER

Harvard University Press   Cambridge, Massachusetts   1973

For Nancy

Apologia

The quintessence of the bureaucrat is accommodation. The instinctive reaction of administrators—deans among them—is to find the answers to questions by balancing off competing arguments, rather than by advocating one or another. Such practices often lessen feckless wrangling within an organization; they also can prevent wise change.

True to my colors as a bureaucrat, I reflect instincts that are conciliatory. Fundamental changes *are* needed in American formal education, yet the resistance to those changes is neither mindless nor conspiratorial. There are reasons why things are as they are. These must be explored dispassionately. Only a clear assessment of where we are and what is possible will indicate what changes are needed. These views place me squarely in the camp of institutional liberals, that newly (and unhappily) despised race. So be it. I am content to rest here.

There is, of course, much in contemporary education to provoke fury. Among our institutions, few depend so mightily on delusion and contradiction as do the schools—and the universities as well, it must fairly be said. The contrast between what we say and what we do is both insufferable and ludicrous. The playing out of these contradictions on small children is, however, immoral, and must stop. Outrage over the suffering of youngsters at our hands is in these respects justified; but outrage unaccompanied by a viable program of remedies rarely leads to reform. Two of the purposes of this book are to expose some of the educational delusions Americans tolerate and to suggest some more honest approaches to formal education than are now in effect. I trust that the instinct to conciliate has not blunted the will to reform.

There is much in the growth and learning of children that we do not understand. Moreover, that part of the craft of teaching which is an art provokes instinctive reactions. One "feels" things to be in or out of order; one gains from the radar fostered (sometimes) through sensitive experience of a kind of sixth sense about children and schools. Many depend on this intuition, myself included. While it rests on no more than (and no less than) subjective judgment, it needs no apologies, and little defense. For much of what we do and should do in education, it is the best we have at hand.

I have tried to see the problem whole. Education is an enormously complex enterprise and requires illumination from many perspectives—psychology, pedagogy, politics, philosophy, law, theology, history, anthropology, and more. To do justice to the problem, one must have a fair grasp of each of these. Few achieve it, certainly not myself. However, the office I have held at Harvard during the last eight years has provided me with a rare opportunity to consider a wide range of issues and to work with a diverse (and remarkable) group of educators. As this experience is fresh, it seems well to capitalize upon it, whatever the risks of superficiality and distortion. Furthermore, I have long protested that too few of my colleagues dare to consider the full range of issues affecting the education of children. Now the cat is belled.

Not surprisingly, I have subtitled this book "speculations." The language I use, however, is assertive, more so than the evidence may warrant. In the interest of arousing my readers, I have deliberately erred on the side of overstatement.

Finally, I have tried to remember that education is as much

concerned with the spirit as with the mind, with qualities of expressiveness as well as with what is expressed. I am intellectually and viscerally antithetical both to the hardheaded analyst who sees education primarily as the collecting of useful skills and to the soft-headed enthusiast of total psychological "awareness." While both have their virtues, the former (often spotted in government agencies) I find a soulless mechanic and the latter (likely to be found in fashionable universities) guilty of gauche parodies of the human spirit. Man is neither a tool to be sharpened nor a flower to be watered. He can learn to discriminate, and he is capable of autonomous love and taste. In a word, he can be civilized. And that is what education, of course, is all about.

T.R.S.

Wrington, Somerset
July 1971

Contents

Places for Learning, Places for Joy

1

Satisfaction

Americans are bored with being told that their educational system is a mess. They have been lectured so often, and with such passion, that one would expect them to be up in arms by now, outraged at what is happening to their young. Not so: their reaction has been disinterest and annoyance. Their children are dying, they are told, and crisis is everywhere. But, with few, brief, noisy, overpublicized exceptions, there has been remarkably little response. The schools change marginally, when at all.

Why? There are several simple reasons. Most Americans are fundamentally satisfied with schools as they are. Most Americans do not listen to the critics carefully enough (if they listen at all) to understand their message. Most Americans distrust the intellectual class from which virtually all the critics are drawn. They want their schools to be conservative, traditional, not the engines of social reform which many critics would have them become. The rhetoric of the reformers has been inflammatory, impolite at best. No one has put forth a comprehensive, politic statement of what might be done to improve the educational system, however good or bad it might now be. The remedies in response to criticism have been piecemeal.

It is, of course, difficult precisely to "prove" this conservatism and satisfaction which is felt by "most Americans."

1

While there have been various studies suggesting this likelihood, the most telling evidence is quite straightforward: if
the majority wanted to change the schools, they would have
done so. On the contrary, support for the schools endures,
and, even as the critics flog education's lack of success, local
board after local board demonstrates its faith in what schools
can do by ever adding functions—drug abuse education, sex
education, studies aimed at lessening juvenile delinquency.
No recent national, state, or local political event has served in
any way to threaten the standing of compulsory education,
and with good reason: politicians at each level of government
know full well the hold that schooling has on the American
people. We criticize it, to be sure: but we know it is a Good
Thing. Radical plans of reform are conspicuous for their
failure to spread widely abroad, and strong criticism for the
lack of impact it has on the mass of voters. One best sees the
effect of satisfaction, then, by what has *not* happened.[1]

Most prominent critics of the last twenty-five years have
been either academicians from pretigious universities or
journalists, persons hardly in the mainstream of middle
America. One thinks of Harvard's James Bryant Conant,
Illinois' and Washington's Arthur Bestor, the Navy's Hyman
Rickover (his part of the naval establishment was brainy and
technological), M.I.T.'s Jerrold Zacharias, Columbia's Jacques
Barzun, SUNY's Edgar Z. Friedenberg, and the ubiquitous
scholar-critics Robert Hutchins, Paul Goodman, and Harold

1. The 1971 Gallup Poll of "The Public's Attitudes Toward the Public Schools"
is illuminating. Nationally, it reports, only 3 percent felt that the curriculum is a
"major problem"; teachers and curriculum were ranked consistently as the
elements of the public schools thought to be the most notably "good." The key
problems mentioned were ones of means and politics—finance, integration/segre-
gation, discipline, facilities, dope/drugs. The question on educational innovation is
revealing. Considering the fact that relatively little is going on, the answers to the
query, "In the schools in your community, do you think too many educational
changes are being tried, or not enough?" are interesting: 22 percent felt "too
many being tried"; 24 percent, "not enough"; 32 percent, "just about right"; 22
percent, "don't know." Satisfaction? Apathy? Clearly a heavy dose of both. The
poll was published as part of the September 1971 edition of the *Phi Delta
Kappan*, pp. 33-48.

Taylor. James Koerner started as an academic and became a freelance writer, joining journalist-critics such as Martin Mayer, Nat Hentoff, Charles E. Silberman, George B. Leonard, and Joseph Featherstone. Christopher Jencks left journalism to join *academe*. Only Ivan Illich is hard to categorize. In recent years, several men who have been teachers of children have become influential: John Holt, Jonathan Kozol, Herbert Kohl, and George Dennison among others. Few, however, have remained in practice; few have had extended experience as professional schoolmen. Indeed, virtually none of the prominent post-World War II critics has come from the main-line ranks of the public-school trade. There are virtually no nationally influential critics who are products of and wholly involved in the system. James Herndon is the exception that proves the rule.

The characteristic tone of their writing is shock. Not having been soaked in what are euphemistically called "the realities" or in the expectations of the school-teaching profession, they were appalled by what they found as they visited schools and asked questions. The titles of some of their books give the flavor of their outrage: *Educational Wastelands; The Diminished Mind; Quackery in the Public Schools; Growing Up Absurd; Our Children Are Dying; Compulsory Mis-Education; Death at an Early Age; Crisis in the Classroom.* Rage is even felt in *Slums and Suburbs*, one of the more important books by the quintessently politic James Bryant Conant.

All the critics—even as they disagree in approach and detail—find American schools sloppy, delivering neither on their expressed promises nor on promises that a democracy might appropriately extract from them. Many find them cruel institutions that not only fail to help children but actually harm them. Some critics attribute this flabbiness, if not the cruelty, to a conspiracy by an "interlocking directorate of educationists," as Arthur Bestor put it in 1954. James Koerner, writing more recently, agrees. The schools are subtly controlled by professional educators, he argues, and

directed toward intellectually soft, socially naive ends. Moreover, the schools are incredibly wasteful, particularly of the
time of children.

More often, the charges have been less of deliberate
conspiracy than of what Silberman terms "mindlessness."
Schoolmen, and laymen, too, have not seriously questioned
what the ends and means of education are, and as a result the
entire apparatus drifts and is periodically but superficially
rationalized in a variety of ways. With no strong and specific
consensus for reform, the present is dominated by past
practices, and, out of inertia, today's schools continue on
yesterday's model.

Or so critics argue. But nothing which costs tens of billions
of dollars a year and which appears prominently in every
public budget at each level of government is likely to be
casually mindless. The enterprise as it is *has* support. Most
Americans do *not* find their schools in crisis. If their children
use them, they are concerned, but this concern leads to but
small, incremental changes. Proposals to alter fundamentally
the process of education meet with considerable public
opposition, as reforming schoolmen from the early progressive era to the present can testify. Fundamental rethinking is
strong stuff for most parents and school boards. In community after community one sees the belief that the schools
that the parents attended were tolerably good, and the
children today should have the same kind of education.
Parents complain about the little things—why Johnny is in
the Bluebirds group rather than the Robins group—but they
support the basic structure. The simplistic moralisms about
the need for civic education and the old-fashioned values
expressed by a Joseph Lee of the Boston School Committee
are made fun of in every eastern Massachusetts university
faculty club, but the persistent Lee was re-elected for scores
of years. His record is more than matched by neighboring
Cambridge's James Fitzgerald, an old style, moralistic conservative who has been re-elected every two years, almost

without break, since 1932. Such men are not elected by those who want to turn the clock ahead.

American schools indisputably enjoy strongly rooted political support. This is not due to an effective professional educators' lobby, for nationally there simply is not one. It results from the satisfaction felt by parents and from the disinterest of most other people. No sense of crisis upsets this disinterest. The people are, on the whole, satisfied.

This assertion will surprise some, in view of the almost daily reports in city newspapers of controversy in and over schools. A closer look will show several points about this agitation, however. It is scattered, and the exception rather than the rule. Considering that over a fourth of Americans are engaged in some sort of formal education, the relative silence on the subject is striking. And when pressure is present, it is often being applied by minority groups who see the schools as one of a number of institutions restricting the future options of their children. More likely than not, however, these groups are protesting a school's failure to deliver on its existing promises; they are not demanding that it fundamentally change its ends. They want the schools to honor and respect and teach their children—that is, to do what Americans of favored classes have traditionally always expected them to do. And, too, black and Spanish-speaking parents are pressing schools not so much because of school failures as because of social failures: the schools are compounding the discrimination of society, and the schools are an institution in which local people have some leverage. This educational agitation is part of general (and long overdue) political activity on the part of minority groups. But it is not the result of any pressing sense of *pedagogical* crisis. Quite the contrary.

Not only is much of the agitation related to race or cultural discrimination, it is focused on political matters. The violence depressingly apparent in an increasing number of schools is found in urban areas with high juvenile delinquency rates and social unrest. Children who are driven to savagery outside of schools not surprisingly carry it inside as well. For them, the schools are targets for cynicism, frustratingly in the way, and the teachers symbols of generally hated authority. The reaction of adults to this outrage is to blame the children rather than the schools: conventional wisdom has the kids at fault, not their teachers. For concerned parents, "community control" is the catchword, and it has no pedagogical counter-part. When community control is achieved, there is little effort put forth toward a fundamental rethinking of the *program* for children. The same old curriculum (if now taught by minority-group teachers) most often prevails. The social studies course may now have an Afro-American slant, but it rests on the same assumptions about the ends and means of civic education as the curriculum that preceded it. The excitement deriving from political victory and the involvement of minority-group professionals and paraprofes-sionals may enliven a school for a time—a kind of politically inspired Hawthorne effect. But basic pedagogical rethinking? Rarely. Political radicals in minority groups are often tradi-tionalists in education. "It worked for The Man. Now let it work for us."

The children, too, are satisfied or apathetic, or both. In recent years there has been unrest in many high schools, but the issues so far have been political rather than pedagogical: concerns over race, personal rights, and conduct. Rarely is there concern over the *program*—what and how children learn. The notable exception, the demand for black studies, is the result of political needs and not of any pedagogical end. Much publicity has been given to the so-called student radical, but his relative numbers are at least as small in secondary schools as in universities, and probably smaller. He is articulate and of the upper middle class, and he is as alienated from the majority of his schoolmates as he is from the society he defies. Because he is colorful, he gets inordi-nate attention from the press. His influence, it appears from his lack of success, is limited indeed. Among his age group, apathy is likely as endemic as among adults.

Perhaps the public is itself "mindless," hopelessly traditional, apathetic, and uncaring about education? Such a conclusion is simplistic, for Americans at a highly generalized level have long taken their schools seriously. One must distinguish, however, between what they say and what they do, between their rhetoric and their actions. Furthermore, one must recognize that schools were founded and are supported for basically *conservative* ends. The real end of American schooling has been purposeful traditionalism. The schools are intended to guard, and to reproduce, the culture. They have been cyclical, in tune (if a generation behind) with majority American mores. They have never been devoted to the creation of any kind of "new social order," as George Counts put it in 1932.

To see the full extent of the conservatism of education, one must view the educational enterprise at three levels. The first and most lofty (and the one most popularly written about) is rhetoric: what leaders and critics say the schools are and should be. The second level is subtler: the real expectations of the society as a whole as to what the schools will produce and how they should operate. The discrepancy between the rhetoric and the expectations fluctuates and is a revealing part of American intellectual history. And, lastly, one must look at the reality of the schools, at what is in fact happening in classrooms with children, not what people say is happening or expect to have happen. A search for this kind of reality involves going beyond slogans and course labels and superintendents' reports and is the most difficult kind of social history to undertake. Who went to school, for how long, and what did he give and receive there?

Educators' and politicians' high rhetoric is easy to come by; the society's real expectations are shadowy; and the facts of life in the typical public school over the years are almost entirely obscured. More is the pity, as an understanding of all three levels is a prerequisite to comprehending the nature of educational change in the United States. Short of this scholarship, one must plunge ahead with what evidence is available, keeping rhetoric and expectation and reality carefully apart. One finds interminably consistent rhetoric and persistent reality—and a steep escalation of expectation.

From the earliest settlement of English North America, formal education played a significant part in the colonists' plans. For pious New Englanders, for the polyglot Middle Colonials, and for adventurer Southerners—especially so for the first—schooling was a brake on the slide toward the barbarism they feared in a strange and hostile new world. On one dimension, a call for a classical grammar school in the wilderness was absurd: Latin, rhetoric, and formal mathematics could not help in building a relevant economy. But on another level, the studious copies of English grammar schools, academies, and universities were highly "relevant," for they preserved beyond the first immigrant generation the crucial, and comforting, symbols of England. Every society needs its verities, and the mixture of science and myth that constituted the programs of the rudimentary schools and remarkable colleges of the North American colonies seemed to colonial leaders to provide them well. Pious teaching and some crude, book-learned technology served as cultural compasses to conduct and life. Or so the rhetoric asserted, and the ruling groups believed.

Eighteenth-century republicans, on the other hand, saw education not only as a bulwark against the barbarism that had frightened the early colonists but also as a means to political unity. Many leaders, John Adams and Thomas Jefferson among them, saw the schools and universities as central edifices in the American political state. Their rhetoric and their hopes were even more commanding than those of the early Puritan colonists. The nineteenth-century men who attempted to carry out this political creed, Horace Mann,

Henry Barnard, Barnas Sears, and the rest, echoed the rhetoric. Mann wrote in 1846:

> I believe in the existence of a great, immutable principle of natural law, or natural ethics—a principle antecedent to all human institutions and incapable of being abrogated by any ordinances of man—a principle of divine origin, clearly legible in the ways of Providence as those ways are manifested in the order of nature and in the history of the race—which proves the *absolute right* of every human being that comes into the world to an education; and which, of course, proves the correlative duty of every government to see that the means of that education are provided for all.
>
> In regard to the application of this principle of natural law—that is, in regard to the extent of the education to be provided for all, at the public expense, some differences of opinion may fairly exist, under different political organizations; but under a republican government, it seems clear that the minimum of this education can never be less than such as is sufficient to qualify each citizen for the civil and social duties he will be called to discharge;—such an education as teaches the individual the great laws of bodily health; as qualifies for the fulfilment of parental duties; as is indispensable for the civil functions of a witness or a juror; as is necessary for the voter in municipal affairs; and finally, for the faithful and conscientious discharge of all those duties which devolve upon the inheritor of a portion of the sovereignty of this great republic.[2]

Such a statement, made in the 1840's, would be suitable in the 1970's with only minor alterations. Schools were to help children to understand their world, to gain a grasp of fundamentals, and to believe in the American creed.

The rhetoric has remained remarkably consistent in the

2. Reprinted in Lawrence A. Cremin, *Horace Mann on the Education of Free Men: The Republic and the School* (New York, 1957), p. 63.

twentieth century, the only change being a new emphasis on minorities within youth—the very poor, the Negro, the immigrant, the crippled, the blind. The formal education available to the typical, that is, majoritarian, American child was now to be accorded to these other groups, and if they needed special preparation as well, they should have it. The schools' ends remained roughly the same, but the means were broadened to include the props for a thoughtful, Americanized life. Schools were to prepare literate citizens who would be equipped to understand their social and familial duties and to perform them well. The school was to pick up where family and apprenticeship left off. It was the agency representing the interest of the state in the shaping of an individual. Too much has been made of the differences in the rhetoric of nineteenth-century and twentieth-century progressive leaders. Given the changes in their respective worlds, their views of the function of formal education are strikingly similar; Jefferson, Mann, and Dewey are interchangeably cited in our day to make essentially the same points. The rhetorical goals are that close. All that is particularly different today is the addition of new student groups—the broadening of provision of schools to allow for mass education—rather than any fundamental alteration of goals.

When one gets beyond the leaders' hopes and looks at the real, if rarely articulated, expectations on the part of the mass of Americans for their schools, one gets a fine sense of the American gift of deliberate self-delusion. Save for an elite—the purveyors of rhetoric—eighteenth- and nineteenth-century American schools offered only the necessary rudiments of literacy, and, on a different level, they were the bestowers of status. The frontiersman feared a different barbarism than did his cultivated spokesman. The less prestigious academies and colleges founded in the nineteenth century were sterile copies of eighteenth-century models, with programs generally whittled down to absurdly short courses: six weeks at Latin, six weeks at ancient history, six weeks at English literature. They provided the symbol, if not the reality, of the "old" official culture. They were hardly bulwarks against impious barbarism, but they did provide, cheaply, a symbolic cachet of "culture" that the rough-hewn Americans admired. Nineteenth-century Americans learned all "important" things, the practical, useful things of life, on the job. You could not harm little children by having them taught how to read in school, or by briefly squirting a bit of irrelevant pseudolearning at them for social ends, but the important things came later and beyond the hands and talents of schoolmasters. Americans were schooled assiduously in the rudiments, and they felt that these rudiments, whether the three R's for children or a minimal grasp of Latin for the college student, were responsibility enough for formal education. The resulting intellectual mediocrity was seen clearly by Tocqueville, who put it in its best light: "if [an observer of Americans] only singles out the learned, he will be astonished to find how rare they are; but if he counts the ignorant, the American people will appear the most enlightened community in the world."[3] Americans schooled many, superficially.

In spite of high rhetoric as well as rapidly increasing school enrollments in the twentieth century, the average American continued to demonstrate little concern for education well through the Depression years. He talked big (or at least did not challenge his leaders when they did) but acted modestly. As many more children went to school and stayed there longer, one might have expected greater public interest in the content and method of schooling, but this was not to be. Save for the excessively publicized pinpricks of the progressives, there is nothing to suggest a popular interest in the functioning of schools other than the most minimal belief in a marginally financed public authority. No contemporary

3. Alexis de Tocqueville, *Democracy in America* (Paris, 1835), ed. Henry Steele Commager (New York, 1947), p. 46.

politician of national note ever made education a significant public issue: no fact is more telling than this about the general low expectations and apathy of the average American toward schools. They were good for the kids: they taught you how to read and about America and culture; if you stayed long enough, they gave you a diploma that had a certain viability in the marketplace. Schools were never fully entrusted with anything of great importance; religion, values at odds with the dominant, liberal white Protestant values, and detailed occupational training were all avoided. Enrollments went up during the Depression due less to a love for learning than to a wish for a warm room, a free lunch, and something to do. Beyond rhetorical banalities, Franklin Roosevelt was silent on the subject of education both as governor of New York and as President. Harry Hopkins was completely unmoved by the endless requests for attention and resources from the U.S. Commissioner of Education of the time, John Studebaker, by the leadership of the NEA, and by the better-known polemicists such as George Counts. When the country was in crisis, the schools became even less of a priority than in calmer times. The rhetoric went on as before: that was harmless and not too costly. But to reconstruct the schools, to give them significant responsibilities for social reform and amelioration, to give them the job of altering or shaping the labor market, was unthinkable. The rudiments, safely and efficiently taught, were a good thing, but they were the limit.

However, as schools began to enroll a significant percentage of the population, they began, inevitably, to serve as a means of sorting manpower. Degrees, or their equivalent, traditionally had bestowed social as well as intellectual status, providing a cachet that many individuals desired. As the labor force became more mobile, however, diplomas, degrees, and certificates took on a new function as a means by which to make the preliminary, crude selection for employment. By the middle of the twentieth century, the high-school diploma was a necessary qualification for many jobs, and the college bachelor's degree for others. The *content* of the courses leading to a certificate was not relevant; what was important was that its holder as likely as not had some grasp of the rudiments and a measure of self-control and perseverance, a fact he had demonstrated by having completed twelve or sixteen years of schoolwork. Schools, then, were expected to "sort" for the economy, but in a highly generalized manner.

Just as Tocqueville suggested the discrepancy between rhetoric and expectation in the early nineteenth century, Herbert Croly wrote in 1909 of a further American delusion.

The American faith in education has been characterized as a superstition, and superstitious in some respects it unquestionably is. But its superstitious tendency is not exhibited so much in respect to the ordinary process of primary, secondary and higher education. Not even an American can over-emphasize the importance of proper teaching during youth; and the only wonder is that the money so freely lavished on it does not produce better results. Americans are superstitious in respect to education rather because of the social "uplift" which they expect to achieve by so-called educational means. The credulity of the socialist in expecting to alter human nature by merely institutional and legal changes is at least equaled by the credulity of the good American in proposing to evangelize the individual by the reading of books and by the expenditure of money and words . . . the American faith in education is by way of being credulous and superstitious, not because it seeks individual and social amelioration by what may be called an educational process but because the proposed means of education are too conscious, too direct, and too "superficial."[4]

4. Herbert Croly, *The Promise of American Life* (New York, 1909), pp. 400, 402.

Croly speaks of the American "tradition of seeking to cross the gulf between American practice and the American ideal by means of education," and he suggests it should be dismissed with a sneer. He felt that there was "no fundamental objection" to the "national faith in the power of good intentions and redistributed wealth." He found Americans too gullible, too persuaded by the rhetoric that schools would accomplish so much. They expected education both to give the society moral uplift and to provide criteria for employment. This, Croly thought, was an excessive burden.

But Croly, too, was gullible. He assumed that the average American did not see the schools as they really were: largely irrelevant institutions quite unrelated to the rhetoric of their leaders. American spokesmen generated high hopes for schools, but these hopes were to be realized with financially limited means. The country could have its cake, it was argued, without paying very much for it at all. The American leaders who persuaded their people that there was no gap between the rhetoric and the reality were not only credulous; they were cynical, and one must put Franklin Roosevelt at the head of the list.

Until World War II, then, most Americans had, considering the resources they put into them, remarkably low expectations for their children's schools; parents were comfortable knowing that their children were learning just what they had learned. Such low expectations led, not surprisingly, to poor financial and political support for public education. Even if political rhetoric remained high, it was a sham, and everyone, including the children, knew it. There was much good talk about loving and respecting the teacher, but one "loved" and "respected" while paying him a low wage and giving him demeaning jobs (such as policing washrooms) in addition to his teaching.

A new kind of expectation arose after World War II, however. The war, more than any technological or scientific event, changed America from a technically based to a scientifically based economy. The country was dominated less and less by the classic American tinkerer, the nimble-minded, clever technologist. Dominance passed to the men who develop new forms of economic power from theory, from mathematical or scientifically based knowledge. To oversimplify, the man in overalls with the toolbox was replaced by the pipe-smoking type gazing at a blackboard covered with figures and abstract formulas. Less colorfully stated, the decade of the fifties saw a rapidly accelerating demand for men not only with basic mathematical and linguistic skills but with the imagination and a capacity for abstract thinking that enabled them to conceive ways to harness new kinds of energy and envisage schematically situations that could not be physically handled and manipulated, as had steam engines or mines or automobiles. The computer was to this society what the steam engine was to the nineteenth century. But a computer economy, unlike an economy based on the steam engine, requires a highly sophisticated work force. The demands placed by the economy's leaders upon universities, upon the places that prepare scientists and abstract thinkers, grew very rapidly, as the soaring budgets of public and private colleges and universities since World War II clearly show.

This change from a technologically based to a scientifically based economy eventually affected the schools. To get a job now, one had to know more in the abstract, book-learning sense. Wits, a strong back, and persistence were no longer all that was required for a better job. Formal educational institutions (whether schools or institutes operated by industry itself) really had to convey something, or their graduates would not be hired or would not be very effective if hired. As is often the case, the extent of this development has been overstated; there will be for the foreseeable future a variety of jobs that some illiterates can productively fill. The number of men and women needed in the semiskilled, technical occupations is not increasing as rapidly as in some other fields, such as government service. Still, the consensus today is that a great deal more than the rudiments taught in school is essential for economic and social survival. The high-school diploma has decreasing symbolic value. Many get it, and often meaninglessly; it is the knowledge that a person has that is of significance. A straw in the wind of these heightened expectations is seen in the recent efforts at the "national assessment" of educational objectives. Bitterly opposed at first, an effort was well under way by the early seventies to review the substantive learning of American children, region by region. The enterprise has growing citizen support and is the first large-scale review of the nation's schools which concentrates on program rather than political or financial concerns. It is an important indication of the shifting interest of the public from the symbols of schooling to its substance.

The vague generalities concerning the virtues of teaching youngsters the American Way and respect for the rights and obligations of others, virtues well attended to by William Holmes McGuffey in the nineteenth century, have taken on new meaning. The effects of congested living have put a premium on the ability to get along and have given new value to certain common codes of conduct, of restraints and privileges. The almost incredible human density not only of our ghettos but of our Levittowns has awakened in Americans subtle new fears and, accordingly, new expectations for schools to relieve those fears. The content of so-called social studies has taken on renewed importance in the 1960's; the public now demands the teaching of socially acceptable behavior. It is not just the escalation of skills needed to survive in the post-World War II economy that has put a strain on the American system; it is the friction caused by close living and the push for civil liberties and civil stability which has given new urgency to school programs.

Even more subtle has been the rise in fear and disillusionment in the average American. Tocqueville found us gullible, Croly saw us as credulous; neither would be correct today. In

the early fifties the American people slowly realized that
World War II was not a war to end all wars but rather a major
skirmish in a generally disoriented world. For the United
Nations, Americans had a high rhetoric and high expectations; the latter had subsided by the 1960's. As assassination
sharpened the political and racial upheavals of the 1960's,
and as the morality of the war in Vietnam came more into
question, Americans were increasingly persuaded that they
lived not in an optimistic society but rather in a "sick" one.
The intellectual community, in particular, engaged in an
unprecedented orgy of national self-flagellation.

At its realistic best, this new attitude may be the beginning
of American maturity. Americans have been as squalid and as
destructive as most people, but, through rhetoric backed by
economic and military might, they have been able to keep
alive the illusion of an American hegemony with moral ends.
As doubt creeps into the American character, however, fear
grows, fear of losing the easy comfort that knowing we were
"right" has provided. The reaction of political left and right
is to turn to education: make us "more moral" or "more
sure" by teaching us this way or that.

To recapitulate: the expectations for education on the part
of the public appear to be rising; and there is cause for
optimism in this. Unfortunately Americans have caught
themselves in a web of assumptions about the operation and
management of schools which retard imaginative steps to act
upon these rising expectations. These assumptions, even
though in some cases blatantly false, adhere almost unchallenged in American perception. They constitute a set of
institutional verities, the public's and the profession's icons.

The first of these verities implies both that there is a
national consensus on the general purposes of education—
which, as rhetoric, is self-evident—and that the specific steps
following from these purposes are clearly understood and, in
fact, in operation—which is not at all self-evident. The ends

of education are no problem, it seems; the only issues are ones of execution. Careful analysis of what schoolmen ought to be seeking is thus replaced by a preoccupation with all sorts of enabling mechanisms, from "performance contracting" and "education vouchers" to "uses of educational technology." There is much dark talk of input and output and throughput and systems and decision-making matrices and accountability, with virtually no detailed review of deep purpose. Explicit goals remain unexamined and hortatory. Periodically, when a statement of ends seems politically propitious, a group of influential persons is assembled to issue a glittering but practically useless paper, usually cast as vaguely as the goals implicitly asserted by "most Americans." Sometimes, rather, an economist is engaged to project current realities into the future, and from these to extract goals. Or a philosopher is summoned to give wisdom, to be an instant Dewey. Rigorous analysis, such as one finds in Benjamin Bloom's *Taxonomy of Educational Objectives* or in Israel Scheffler's elegant analyses of teaching, is notable both for its scarcity and for its lack of influence on policymakers. The people believe they are together on the purposes of education. But they do not see nor do they want to see inconsistencies in, for example, the clash between corporate and individual aspirations. Worse yet, they are condescending about the problem. Anyone who is concerned with goals is, inevitably, an impractical, dull type: of course, we all know that education is simply what goes on in schools. Thus do Americans pile educational policy on top of the delusion that we know precisely what we want to accomplish.

The second verity can be simply put: Formal Education is a Good Thing, and the more you have of it the better you are. Education is primarily *quantitative*, not qualitative. One attends school, rather than learns something. One collects the symbols, diplomas, and degrees, and these are evidence not only of accomplishment but of virtue. Men with Education are Good Men. One becomes a Good Man by attending a school and a university. Attendance is the heart of the matter.

The third icon is compulsion: everyone, at least up to a certain age, *must* attend school. Formal education is such a Good Thing that everyone, willy-nilly, must do time in a school building. Why this is so is obvious: School is where one learns Important Things. Children should learn Important Things. Therefore, children should go to School.

The fourth verity is the public school itself, though this icon has cracks in it. Some families, almost exclusively for religious reasons, prefer a nonpublic school (which, however, is assiduously modeled, on all but doctrinal matters, on its public counterpart). Most Americans, however, believe that all children should go to the same kind of school, a school run by a public authority and financed with public funds. "Public" in fact means government-operated. A school which is privately managed but which is a burden on the public purse (through tuition, or indirectly through tax relief) is a "private" school. The public interest requires public management, it appears.

The pattern of ownership and operation of schools that was in effect throughout most of American history—a public charter, independent management, and financial support by the government—is rare in contemporary elementary and secondary education, though it is prevalent in higher education. Several privately managed universities receive the lion's share of their operating funds from the government. Harvard, blessed with a private endowment of over one billion dollars and with fiercely independent governing bodies, was created by government charter and, at Independence, had its legal existence sanctioned by a clause in the state constitution. Today it receives some forty percent of its annual revenues from the federal government alone. Harvard may be privately managed, but it is very much a public university in the sense that it spends government money and allocates this in ways mandated by public authorities. The

Universities of Pennsylvania and Pittsburgh combine public funding and independent government; Cornell follows still another pattern. And there are many other variations. Yet no such eclecticism exists in the schools. Conventional wisdom holds that there should be one public school, and this operated by public authority. Any alternative is regarded not just as inappropriate but as treason. Critics who have suggested quite mild versions of voucher experiments, for example, to promote diversity in schools, have been attacked violently—which is hard to explain in rational terms.

This excess of emotion is related to the fifth verity: the role of the public school as a shaper of the American mind. As Lawrence Cremin has written, "I myself am led to the conclusion that the nurture of a common culture remains a central task of American popular education, and that the common school continues to stand as a prime agency for undertaking this task." The school, he points out, is not the social and ethnic melting pot that conventional wisdom has us believe it is; and the educational media—radio and television—cannot see any systematic educational task through. Cremin's concept of popular culture includes both intellectual ability and a sensitivity to American liberal idealism and taste. His viewpoint is unashamedly utopian; as he optimistically asserts, "the case for popular education rests on the proposition that culture can be democratized without being vulgarized. It is a radical proposition that flies in the face of two thousand years of Western wisdom to the effect that true culture demands an elite. And it is a proposition that must really be accepted on faith, since the whole idea of a democratic culture is too new to have stood the test of time."[5] To the extent that intellectual *discrimination* is at the heart of a high democratic culture (as indeed it must be), then a school is an appropriate site for labor toward that end. And to that extent at least, education should be a homogeni-

5. Lawrence A. Cremin, *The Genius of American Education* (Pittsburgh, 1965), pp. 75, 78.

zing influence. But the transmission of common values by the schools raises difficult problems.

In their most simplistic (and therefore most dangerous) form, these values are already the staple of the commercial media. Americans like to watch programs that reinforce, rather than challenge, the majority ethic. At their most profound and sophisticated, these values can rarely be inculcated in the abstract, in conventional schools; they must be experienced in richly diverse settings. Schoolrooms are simply not the most effective places to dispense values such as are embodied in the best of (in Gunnar Myrdal's phrase) an American Creed. The noblest aspect of the American liberal tradition is its respect for diversity. And this is not very likely to be fostered in a single setting, a unitary schoolhouse. Be that as it may, however, Cremin's argument that the school must be an agent of cultural cohesion is far more sophisticated than the majority's iconographic verity. For most Americans, the school's task is to teach the American way—which is, in fact, uncritical, chauvinist, and Protestant.

This fifth verity conflicts sharply with the sixth, which is the widely held faith in locally controlled education. The schools are there to teach the American way, but they must be controlled by the individual community as a protection from values that might be imposed by a central authority. The critic may reasonably ask: are there national values, or aren't there? Schools are, in the conventional wisdom, melting pots; yet they must be autonomously run by the individual neighborhoods, which are usually class- and race-segregated. Do Americans want melting pots or segregated schools? The cynic must conclude that they want the first but under the guise of the second.

States have virtually unchallenged authority in education; counties or municipalities have the virtually unchallenged delegated authority to maintain the schools. Is education really a state concern, or isn't it? Community control is endorsed by most state leaders ("keep education close to the people"), but what constitutes a "community" (its size and composition)? Horace Mann's arguments in favor of a decentralized system of education is used today to defend a policy of centralization in the "town" of Boston, which today has a school population as large as that of Mann's Massachusetts. Whatever the current unit of control, the passions aroused in its favor are fiery: the political status quo in education has considerable resilience. Not surprisingly, doubletalk and deception over supposed issues of control are rife. Single-minded integrationists argue for metropolitan school systems primarily on economic grounds. Equally single-minded segregationists defend localism on traditional, political grounds. And most Americans assert, however speciously, that the schools must be "close to the people," and to them that means some kind of localism. The pedagogical virtues and vices of localism are rarely even considered. School politics appear to have little concern with education or children.

The seventh verity is that the public schools do not teach religion but do teach values. As we have pointed out, this distinction, save at the obvious extremes, is not valid. The public schools do not blatantly inculcate sectarian doctrine, and they do teach many subjects that are unrelated to questions of the spirit, subjects that might be termed ethically secular. But organized religion permeates our history, art, and literature; one cannot teach social studies or the humanities without going into religious explanations. Ethical, even theological questions are so close to the children that teachers cannot, responsibly, avoid dealing with them. The manner in which teachers and students treat one another, the extent of their mutual trust and charity, implicitly teaches values, many of which can properly be called religious values. The limits of any secular morality are indeed narrow. Yet the illusion of a strict separation between church and state is maintained. The law is full of arguments at each extreme, on how and where and what doctrine and denominational practice can be promulgated. And the subtler and actually far more significant role of the religious *spirit* in education is ignored. Schools should teach social and political morality, conventional wisdom has it, but never religion; and there is a sharp line between them. This obfuscation leads to inconsistent and distorted teaching in the schools and brings confusion to the children's minds.

The eighth verity concerns another separation, that between school and politics. At one level, this is sensible practice: the schools should be insulated from short-term political wars and from patronage. On another level, however, this is simply wrongheaded. The educational development of a child cannot be neatly separated from his physical development or his style of life. Education, health, housing, city planning, transportation, and such all are woven together in the child's experience. For society to influence any one without careful reference to the others is as inefficient as it may be harmful to the child. The need to coordinate social and cultural services is blatant, but disregarded all too often. On still another level, the separation between education and politics is both absurd and unwise. No institution supported from tax revenues can or should be above politics. No official responsible for carrying out legislative or constitutional mandates should be exempt from being held publicly accountable. No mayor or city council responsible for setting tax rates can legitimately waive his obligations toward education (too many do, and they get away with it, the verity being as persistent as it is). Moreover, the substance of education is, in several fundamental aspects, a matter of politics. "Let us make republican machines," intoned Benjamin Rush more than a hundred and fifty years ago; the early nationalists knew well what ideology they wished the schools to impart.[6] At least some of them, like Rush, were honest about it. We dispense a similar kind of democratic chauvinist ideology in

6. Benjamin Rush, "Thoughts upon the Mode of Education Proper in a Republic" (1786), in Frederick Rudolph, ed., *Essays on Education in the Early Republic* (Cambridge, Mass., 1965), p. 17.

schools today but pretend that this has nothing to do with partisan political beliefs. Americans assume that a wall exists between the rough and tumble of political life and the cool rationality of the academy and the schools. The effects of this illusion are as capricious as those of the separation of church and state.

The final verity arises from the retrospective character of education. Schools, conventional wisdom has it, are to pass on the inherited traditions of the culture. Schools are to make men of children. Schools are to teach what the parents believe and to prepare the children for the careers that their parents now pursue. At the same time, schools are to prepare the young for the future, for earthly conditions as they will be, not as they were, for manhood appropriate to a future rather than a present time, for values relevant to the inevitably changing conditions that will obtain two or four or more decades hence. It is assumed that the latter ends will be achieved by practices emerging from the former. There is a naive belief that historical study will *inevitably* prepare a child for a future society (though school rarely asks him to attempt a disciplined, abstract leap forward). Today's mode of life—the nuclear family, one or at most two careers, and pronounced splits between work and leisure and between male and female—is perceived as the *inevitable* future norm. Alternative likelihoods are rarely examined. Current values are presumed to be everlasting; radically different prospects such as supranational government and a fairer division of wealth among nations are rarely considered, much less seriously studied. Contemporary employment practices and job skills will simply be carried on, bigger and better; the strong likelihood of a radical change in employment styles in a post-industrial society is barely addressed. Schools, in brief, are to teach Johnny what Dad was taught, and also to prepare Johnny for the future. The inherent inconsistency in the goals is persistently ignored.

Unhappily, Americans steadfastly cling to these crippling verities while their hopes and expectations continue to rise. To confuse the situation even further, moreover, various interest groups within the society stake out special claims, particular expectations for education. While most of these are obvious, the conflicts among them are traditionally ignored, and only add to the confusion that makes up American perceptions of education.

Nation and state have similar claims. Both need citizens who willingly meet minimal social responsibilities (both understanding and obeying the law, voting and acting in a principled fashion), who are competent and thus able to support themselves and their dependents, and who are adaptable in that they can move readily from one geographical region or from one line of work to another. Given the constitutional responsibility of states to provide formal education, they have a special claim that it be carried out effectively and efficiently. The county, metropolitan area, or city has still more specific claims, that the manpower needs of each region be met and that the educational system be sufficiently uniform to accommodate the migration of children from school to school within the area. It is also required that schools be orderly and operated at as low a cost as is politically feasible.

The immediate community, the village or neighborhood, has its own special concerns. The school should reflect its values: children's commitment and obedience to the life style of the community should be reinforced, not challenged. A predominately progressive, intellectual community, for example, usually wants a highly competitive setting, full of academic rough and tumble (though, paradoxically, packaged in traditional ways), a school with a modish, cosmopolitan flair. A stable working-class community wants a school that reaffirms for its children the values of hard work and the inevitable rewards that come to those who apply themselves, a school which honors traditional virtues and frowns on topical fads. A frightened minority community wants a school that gives its children the skills they need to survive in a hostile society, usually skills of a highly traditional, academic sort, a school which, too, dignifies the minority's ethic and gives the community a renewed sense of pride. A neighborhood that values racial integration wants its schools harmoniously integrated. A community that wants to keep to itself wants a school which preserves that condition and accommodates it satisfactorily within its teaching of the American way. Some communities will value a school which promotes the child's chances to improve himself, to do better than his parents. This Horatio Alger ideal is presumably a part of that community's ethic—the wish among the modestly endowed for great success—and represents no challenge. Alger, of course, worked within the system. In addition, the school should respond to local pressures and needs; it should help curb local juvenile hooliganism, for example, serve as a neighborhood center, provide sports entertainment, and be an institution to be proud of. Neighborhoods like to think they have good schools, and not always for civic reasons. Good schools raise real-estate values and draw the attention of business. Good schools mean a stable community.

Most parents, obviously, have claims similar to those of the neighborhood. A few might be opposed to local values and want the school to, if not teach children to challenge the status quo, at least not punish the child who does so. Above all, however, parents want the assurance that the schools will reflect their ideals and their hopes for their children. They also want their children protected, in a literal, physical sense. And, most obviously, they want the schools to give their child the skills to get ahead (though parents sometimes differ widely on what those are). Most parents want their children to do well in school and to get high grades, not only to get ahead but for their own sake. Parents derive a vicarious thrill from the triumphs of their children.

Employers have claims, too. Quite naturally, they want to hire young people who are at least partially trained; the more vocationally relevant study the school can offer, the less the employer has to provide at his own expense. Employers expect schools to teach those virtues. Some employers place special weight on the individual's flexibility; many lines of work require artisans and workmen of great adaptability. There is much talk, in these businesses, of some sort of "general" vocational education, to be provided by schools.

Sectarian religious groups want to reach children, too; they want an atmosphere in the public schools which neither mocks nor undermines formal religious activity. They want a climate of religiosity, the schools reinforcing the expectation that families will be part of one church or another. Schools should help children to believe in God. As the supposedly secular pledge of allegiance which millions of schoolchildren repeat daily holds, we are "one nation, under God, indivisible . . . "

The teachers constitute a special and increasingly influential estate. Their claims are as predictable as they are understandable. Teachers long for respect and the autonomy that follows from it. They want the limits of their professional domain clearly outlined and their essential authority within it assured. They want physical, psychological, and economic protection. (No one enjoys threats and invective, whether from adults or from children; and no one likes to be in financial straits, or in fear of losing his job.) They want a system that recognizes and rewards talent, but they want to police themselves. Organized teachers are an interesting combination of the classic trade union (a mass organization devoted primarily to group protection) and the classic profession (a small, highly trained group which maintains its autonomy through the respect and importance accorded its expertise).

And the children? Each has the right to learn, to be competent and discriminating, the right to be himself, to be critical and independent, the right to privacy and to protection from other individuals and groups, including teachers, the right to learn skills that someone else values enough to pay for. Few youngsters would put these claims so boldly; the sad cynicism of many of them would not allow it. The bored and resigned just wait to get out of school. They ask only to be bothered as little as possible.

Peoples' rising expectations, then, are caught in web upon web of inherited, rarely examined tradition and the special interests of particular social and political groups. While some of the increased demand of schools arises from newly felt doubt about the American system, this doubt has not yet served to shake belief in the several "verities" of school practice, nor has it illumined the conflicts between the expectations of self-interested groups. Many of us want new wine, it seems; but we assume that it will go into old bottles.

Given the durability of American views of school practice, it is no surprise to find that, with but few exceptions, school programs have altered little since the 1890's. Considering the prodigious changes in American society since 1900, it is remarkable, and not merely the result of chance, that only minor rearrangements have been seen. The opportunities for schooling have broadened to include a larger group of people, inaugurating a policy of mass education; yet what we give the majority of children on both elementary and secondary levels has remained largely the same.

While both the percentage of Americans attending school and the numbers involved grew rapidly (at times almost geometrically), what was taught and how it was taught did not change. We grouped children by age in 1900; we still group them that way today. Children were taught in clusters of twenty to forty and are still taught essentially the same way. In 1900 schools were organized around a virtually autonomous teacher responsible for about thirty students;

the same is true today. The principal pedagogy in 1900 was an assignment from the text, the reading and partial memorizing of this text, the performance of certain exercises from the text either on paper with pencil or orally in class, followed by some limited discussion and a test; the same practice is followed today. The amount of time both in the elementary and in the secondary grades allotted to the staple subjects—English and languages, mathematics, social science in one form or another, and natural science—has remained relatively stable. The newer subjects, for example, vocational and commercial education, still affect a relatively small number of students, and for a minor portion of their school training.

In 1885 the city of Chelsea, Massachusetts, asked President Charles William Eliot of Harvard to design for its high schools a curriculum that was up-to-date and atuned to current scholarly and university standards. He organized a four-year curriculum, with English (including some historical material), mathematics, and natural science at its core. Those planning to complete high school took three years of Latin; others took more English or French. Greek or German were available electives. Gym, art, and music were added in small doses. This is in essence not very different—not as different as one would expect, considering the changed circumstances—from the program suggested nationally in 1959 by another president of Harvard, James Bryant Conant. The "main-line" subjects—language, mathematics, science, and social science (largely history)—predominate.

One can say, of course, that the titles of courses do not give the whole picture, and that is at least partially right. However, it is instructive to read the transcripts and descriptions of elementary- and secondary-school classes of fifty years ago and then to visit the schools of today. The similarities in the form of instruction, the relationship between pupils and teachers, and the ways schools are run are striking. At the turn of the century, schools emphasized form and the manner of doing things; they still do so today. By any definition, there has been amazingly little change.

This assertion runs counter to the reproach, heard in the 1950's, of progressive education, particularly of John Dewey. Much of this criticism was misplaced: it should have been directed at the traditions of American elementary and secondary education affirmed and institutionalized in the 1890's. Some scholars exalt the patterns of the 1890's, but in so doing they misread both the actual functioning of schools in that period and the realities of schools in their own time.[7]

But progressivism should have its due. A significant number of additional people attended the schools. Equally important, a new intellectual climate enveloped education, and various new approaches, such as psychological testing, made their appearance and had their impact. For college admission, psychological testing replaced the separate achievement testing that the colleges themselves had employed in the nineteenth century, and, in an important sense, increasingly standardized the secondary-school curriculum. Such a standardization was developing of its own accord in any event, but the testing movement accelerated it. Psychological inquiry and psychoanalysis enabled scholars to look at teaching and learning in new ways and to draw new conclusions about differences among individual children and groups of children, and about the effects of teacher authority on children.

The progressive movement created places in school for the mass of American children, but it provided only a new rhetoric, not a new program. One now had "social studies" rather than "history," yet the substance of the subject was historical. Exciting, separate "model" schools were established, but their dogmas rarely spread, except rhetorically. New scientific scholarship created new insight into learning, but there was little success in translating this insight into

7. See my *Secondary Schools at the Turn of the Century* (New Haven, 1964), chapter 4.

pedagogical   strategies and techniques that would affect large numbers of children. Thus, both the model schools and the scholars had limited effect on school practice in classrooms. The energies of school managers were directed toward surviving the opening of enough schools to accommodate the floods of children pouring in. The past fifty years have not been a time for basic reconstruction and reconsideration of the nature of education and the content of schooling. We accepted the 1890 model and applied it on an ever-increasing scale. For the majority of American children, neither the substance nor the method of schooling has changed significantly since 1900.

The changelessness of the content of schooling is a striking fact of American social history of the last fifty years, and may not have been a bad thing for Americans at all. It is not enough, however, to curse or applaud this tendency in schooling; it is important to understand why a resistance to change exists, so that a realistic attempt can be made to alter what we feel should be altered.

But there is more to the conservatism of schools, for the teaching profession is itself conservative. Upwardly mobile lower-middle-class persons, the core of the present teaching profession, are rarely boatrockers, and they, more than any other group, form the basis of the resistance to change. They themselves were, of course, good representatives of the "typical American," the man of tradition, worshipper of symbols. In addition, large numbers of teachers were (and are) women, many of them short-timers with major concerns elsewhere. Satisfaction for them did not hinge on the job and doing it well, but rather on families and careers outside of teaching. Many simply served, and are serving, their time with as little effort at change as possible. Moreover, with large numbers of teachers leaving the profession each year—in the 1950's, one out of five left annually—it was hard to build a continuing base for reform.

One such base could have been the teacher-education

institutions, but the traditions of their staffing militated against this. Most normal schools, teachers' colleges, and schools of education were staffed by former teachers, persons experienced and successful in their craft who saw their task as passing along their accumulated wisdom. These are not the people to lead dramatic reform movements (though, as the English have found, there are exceptions). The teachers' colleges did much to give the profession its ingrown quality as well as desirable esprit. Ingrownness had its virtues: teachers organizations have certain warm and useful clubiness about them. The people who became teachers, then, were instinctively conservative. Also, the way the enterprise was organized and the way men and women moved in and out of it discouraged change. The teacher-training institutions and the professional organizations in fact reinforced conservative tendencies already there.

Little was done by the education industry, particularly the purveyors of textbooks, to foster reform. Most textbook publishing houses were marginal business operations, operating on narrow profits. The highly scattered educational market required a costly sales force and entailed considerable risks, and few publishers mounted research and development programs on a scale seen in other American industries. Moreover, the textbook trade understandably aimed its products at the buyers, the largely conservative teachers. Although ostensibly school committees and state authorities had control over the selection of textbooks, often it was the educators who made the choice. At no point did the private citizen take a decisive lead in developing new approaches and opening up new directions.

There was never a core of realistic, sufficiently ruthless leaders to generate the necessary changes. The leaders' leader was, of course, John Dewey, but for most teachers his writing and thinking was distant and opaque. His interpreter, William Heard Kilpatrick, spoke in terms which for many were largely irrelevant and impractical. George Counts was a stimulating visionary; most of his ideas, although applauded by many teachers, were never put into practice. The private and parochial schools, while making much of their supposed independence to experiment, either failed to do so or did so under such special circumstances and with such special children that it had little relevance for the masses.

Scholarship, particularly in psychology and the related behavioral sciences, rarely had an engineering component. Few psychological theories have been formulated in terms that can be used by large numbers of people. Edward Thorndike and his colleagues in the mental testing movement clearly developed techniques employable by (or rather, on) the mass of children. In actual teaching (in contrast with evaluation), the programmed-instruction movement initiated by B.F. Skinner is almost unique. Most scholars have ignored what Skinner recognized: the necessity to translate scholarly findings into forms useful to and usable by persons of limited training and imagination. Furthermore, much of the educationally relevant research that was done was either trivial or removed from useful application. As a result, the new ideas being developed during the progressive period found little expression except at the periphery of education.

Underlying all these conditions is the fact that American expectations about schooling change very slowly. The rhetoric notwithstanding, it was not until very recently, and even then only sporadically, that Americans began to expect something more from their schools than that they provide rudimentary skills, pass along certain cultural verities, and confer status and gauge employability. These ends are all retrospective: except for training in rudimentary skills (which has a certain timeless quality), they *depend* on the past. Traditions, by definition, require history. The symbolic role of education must have stable coinage, a relatively unchanging set of standard values. These public brakes on educational reform are far more important than any "conspiracy" of educators (whom a modestly aroused public could brush aside with ease). Neither is the public "mindless." Its real expectations have been modest and conservative, and it is real expectations that lead to the allocation of money. The educational system is, therefore, modest and conservative. The average American child today gets an education not unlike that accorded his grandmother, because that is what his elders want him to have. But perhaps Granny's education isn't good enough.

One can *explain* why schools have resisted change and have served traditional social ends, but that does not mean that the condition is a happy one. There is a crisis in American education precisely because most Americans are quietly satisfied with their educational institutions, and deluded by its icons. By any dispassionate judgment, the country's educational system is not fulfilling even the modest objectives expected of it.

The crisis takes several forms. The system teaches the rudiments tolerably well to those of lower-middle income and above. Perhaps these children would learn anyway, from sources outside school; but, lacking evidence to that effect, we give the schools the credit. The system does provide some of the symbols of culture, as anyone who has recently attended a high-school graduation can testify. As the number of youths graduating from high school approaches ninety percent, however, the usefulness of the diploma for employment diminishes. Yet it becomes more and more difficult for the high-school dropout to break into even semiskilled occupations. The schools do keep the children off the streets (some of the time) and out of the labor market (most of the time). These expectations are being reasonably well met for the majority of Americans.

American rhetoric and some growing popular expectations go beyond this, however. The schools are expected to be the primary vehicles to "give kids a chance," to provide all youngsters with the skills and attributes required to "make

it" in the economy and in society. Recent evidence overwhelmingly demonstrates that schools do *not* provide youngsters with a fair means to social mobility. The often quoted
"Equality of Educational Opportunity" study, the so-called
Coleman Report, most recently showed that academic
achievement, as the profession and public now define it,
correlates with income: the wealthier your parents are, the
more likely you are to score high on tests. The schools, then,
reinforce class structures: they legitimize, in an apparently
objective manner, existing social arrangements.

Perhaps the children of wealthy parents really are intellectually more capable than the children of poor parents, but
the consistency of correlated achievement and income data is
too bold to ignore. There are, obviously, many intellectually
able children among low-income groups: clearly, the schools
are failing to identify a significant number of them and to
move them forward academically. If one believes that intellectual capability has no correlation at all with parental
income (and this belief is a part of American rhetoric), then
the failure of the schools is all the more blatant. The schools
do *not* provide the basis for a classless meritocracy. Indeed,
with few exceptions, they never have.

Moreover, the tests used to measure achievement—the tests
that control the gateway to the diploma and status—may well
be class- and culture-biased. Most tests, particularly those set
by teachers (rather than by professional testers), use language; the linguistically inept score low. But are they, by that
token, stupid and without promise? One doesn't know; one
only knows that they cannot read and write very well.
Ability, clearly, takes many forms. But society's principal
sorting system, formal education, rewards one kind of intellectual ability almost exclusively—language. Other abilities
rarely count; and since low-income groups almost by definition live in language-poor environments—those in which
fewer words are used than in comparable middle-class settings, and many of these words are not words sanctioned by

the "official culture"—these youngsters are at a disadvantage. For confirmation, one need only look at the low-income groups who "made" it: the Jews, in particular, even recently arrived immigrants, are raised in language-rich homes, environments that clearly reinforce the "official" standards. The system depends, clearly, on the use of middle-class language.

Schools, then, do not give lower-income children the tools to become middle-class children (defined primarily in terms of language ability). Of course, some low-income youngsters might, quite properly, not want to become middle-class children. They may want to worship at different altars and be rewarded for different talents. This is, theoretically, a fine proposition: schools should reward a variety of talents— linguistic, mathematical, aesthetic, manual, and more. But this is meaningless unless the society, too, rewards these talents, and there are few indications that it does. To "make it" as an artist, for example, one must also "make it" in conventional terms. Middle-class values may be cursed, but they are the values held by most Americans, and this majority controls the society and the routes up within it. The only hope for broader standards is to make cultural diversity a part of the middle-class ethic. Assault on the middle class does not work, as everyone from Newton Minow to Martin Luther King found. Joining, and then reshaping, the majority class might. But until that happens, the fact remains that schools are dominated by the middle class; the children of the comfortably well-off succeed in it because the schools reflect their values; the children of the poor rarely make it in an educational sense. Schools are not melting pots; they legitimize the social status quo.

Given the amount of schooling they received, Americans ought to be "most enlightened," as Tocqueville put it. Each now spends at least two thousand full days in the classroom before the age of eighteen. But in spite of this Americans remain monumentally gullible, susceptible to the boldest trickery. As J.K. Galbraith points out, the producer of goods can now *create* demand, rather than merely responding to it. The large American corporation can, at least in part, control the full commercial circle: materials, production, *and* market. As a result, the free-enterprise system no longer works, for the marketplace is not reacting to the real needs of con- sumers but to needs created by the producer. The advertising industry rides on the public's gullibility, of course; it depends on it. We can be persuaded to want many things. We are easily trapped by non sequiturs: Pepsi-Cola making us young again, Chryslers making us powerful, deodorants making us wholesome. We are too often taken in by the classic rapier of Madison Avenue: "If you don't use   , you won't be   "; the blanks can be filled in almost at random, and without regard for logic.

Once again, Americans get what they deserve. If they wanted logical sales practices, they could demand them. But consumerism is a minority crusade in the United States and is led by reformers similar in background and style to edu- cational critics and having no broader political or professional base than they do. The merchandising system works well enough; its efficiency is comforting: it demonstrates that we *can* change behavior. But *we haven't been schooled to see the cheating, the slick lying, the self-serving innuendos.* In a word, we lack discrimination.

To be gulled by merchants is one thing: to be gulled in politics is quite another. Presidents are "sold." This is not new, of course; Andrew Jackson was sold. What is new is the immense leverage that mass-communications technology can exert. The potential for controlling political behavior is much greater now than ever. Yet, although Americans are schooled far longer today than in Jackson's time, they are, it would seem, no less susceptible to political imagery. They tolerate lies and are trapped by appearances. No man who was ugly or projected a disagreeable image could become President; nor could one who could not advertise. Nixon "lost" the 1960 debates with John Kennedy. A Humphrey TV blitz ten days earlier might have swung the 1968 election. Americans are convinced that there is a meaningful distinction between ground fighting and airborne fighting in Cambodia and Laos. They find, seemingly, no inconsistency in a policy that takes farm lands out of production in the face of world starvation. And so forth. The average American is schooled, to be sure; but he is not very sharp at making distinctions. He is a pushover for political and business interests. An ideal democracy would ensure that its people be able to think clearly and to make wise choices. That ours does not is a tragedy, the stuff of the deepest crisis in American education.

And yet, ironically, we are in all satisfied with our schools.

2

Ends

A majority of Americans agree now, as they have in the past, on three simple purposes for education—purposes which, while progressive and useful, are so obvious and accepted that they seem hackneyed. They are not true clichés, of course, for they are often honored only in the breach. They are cast very broadly, and there are countless ways of expressing their generality in specifics and countless means to achieve those specifics. Among them, contradictions, friction, and even the possibility of reform emerge.

It is generally agreed that every person should have individual *power*, the maximum use of his intellectual and physical faculties for personal and corporate ends. He should be able to understand, to select, and to act in a purposeful, deliberate manner.

Secondly, everyone should have what might be called a sense of *agency*, the personal style, assurance, and self-control that allow him to act in both socially acceptable and personally meaningful ways. He should have a sense of himself, a personal vision, however fanciful or humble; and he should find a minimally compromised way of accommodating that vision to cultural tradition and immediate social reality. The culture itself has legitimate claims on the individual, and a society should see that these are impressed upon each citizen. The individual does not have anarchic freedom;

and the culture does not have total authority. A balance appropriate to both must be developed—and redeveloped, as such an accommodation must be continuous. A person's sense of agency, then, emerges from the balance between his own vision and social norms.

Thirdly, every person deserves *joy*, the fruit of aesthetic discipline, of faith, and of commitment. The human animal laughs, and wonders, and, in common with some other mammals, he is capable of love. These qualities are not forms of power, really; they are forms of freedom and are human rights. They do not arise wholly from chance, however. They emerge, or are held back, at least in part by design. Every individual has a right to joy and thus to a society designed to enhance it.

Looked at closely, these classic chestnuts of American educational rhetoric are seen to be fraught with contradictions, yet at the same time they are the creatures of history. These ends—especially the first two—were part of Jefferson's rhetoric. But his specific definition and the imperatives of his time gave them, in fact, different meaning. The Constitution itself is partly a cliché: many of its rhetorical verities are self-evident; but the specific meanings are always in a state of flux.

Rhetorical verities are magnificently useful, of course, as they provide a firm point of departure in the formulation and practice of social policy. A wise leader moves from them, developing specific aims and means to achieve these aims in keeping with the expectations of a majority of citizens. If he is clever as well as wise, he casts his means in policies that appropriately raise, or wisely alter, these expectations. A constitutional prince might advise: assert a widely accepted verity; assert a policy to forward that aim, but develop a specific means which, in execution, gives a new and better definition to that aim. This is a credo of liberal democracy; and, given the mass character and popular commitment to education, it is a most pragmatic approach to educational policy. Those who wish to improve society avoid considerations of the "aims of education"—cultural rhetoric and social expectations—at their peril.

Alfred North Whitehead gave a classic, if unlovely, definition of educated *power*: "the acquisition of the art of the utilization of knowledge."[1] An individual has mental and physical faculties which can be put to use for his benefit and for the benefit of others. Many of these faculties develop most quickly and effectively when nurtured. Ergo, formal education. Others have defined educated power in similar ways. A.H. Halsey wisely remarked that "an educated man is one who knows how to get around his ignorance." For Howard Mumford Jones, an educated man is one who can separate wise men from fools. In a current idiom, for Neil Postman and Charles Weingartner the educated man is the one equipped with "crap detectors," sensitive radar that can separate the pearls from the goo that inevitably envelops them.[2] In other words, an educated man, among other things, can *discriminate*.

Discrimination is not only analysis; it is an approach. Call it logic, or science, or systematic deliberation: It is a process of intellectual selection based on facts or on evidence educed from whatever facts are available. It is disciplined inquiry, whether into the age of a prehistoric human jawbone or into the properties of an alloy or into the facts of an argument at law. It is also humbler inquiry, such as assessing which soap powder on a supermarket shelf is in fact the least expensive per pound or which candidate for city council is the lesser rogue. It is the process of inquiry which makes discrimination possible.

No process can stand alone; there must be facts to sustain it. What facts a person knows will necessarily color his process of analysis. One can make elegant and logically

---

1. Alfred North Whitehead, *The Aims of Education* (New York, 1929), p. 6.
2. Halsey's and Jones's remarks are from informal discussion. Postman and Weingartner write in *Teaching as a Subversive Activity* (New York, 1969).

consistent arguments from incorrect or irrelevant data, as those who have studied medieval theology, contemporary politics, and Perry Mason court trials know all too well. Some kinds of facts must be part of every individual's analytic equipment. In addition, the process of inquiry should have within it not only a respect for accuracy but the means of locating new facts.

Herein lies a major problem, for all too many educators have exalted the facts above the process of discovering their meaning—which, of course, is the heart of the matter. The substance of reality, while endless, is easier to organize and teach than are ways of dealing with it. Throughout the centuries, certain substance, certain facts—flyspecks on an endless wall of data—have emerged as the "content" of education and have been legitimized by the mandarins of scholarship. Some of this is essential equipment for the modern discriminating individual; but when miserably taught (as happens all too often), it is not tied in, either in the classroom or in the child's mind, with the process of intellectual inquiry and analysis. It remains simply as Gradgrind rampant: Facts, Facts, Facts.

The balance between process and substance has been a paramount question in educational criticism and debate since World War II. The three most influential critics in the 1950's were Arthur Bestor, then professor of history at the University of Illinois, Admiral Hyman Rickover of the United States Navy's submarine service; and James Bryant Conant, chemist, ambassador, and president of Harvard University. Bestor's acid and outraged *Educational Wastelands* was a reaction to the "powerless" students pouring into higher education after the war—able young men and women, but without the minimal use of their faculties. They lacked discrimination; they lacked the simplest understanding of logical analysis, even the rudimentary facts that support elementary political or scientific analysis. And they lacked the basic communication skills needed to debate and to assert the results of analysis. This condition was intolerable to Bestor; he zeroed in on high schools, which were, to him, sloppy and misdirected. His scapegoats were the leaders of those schools, the "educationists." (His scathing and sarcastic use of that word has made it an American pejorative. In England, an "educationist" is still simply a student of the process of education, wise or stupid.)

Bestor himself showed no confusion over the separate claims of process and content, over an intellectual approach to inquiry and the facts embodied within that inquiry, but several of his imitators did. Bestor, in essence, agreed with Charles W. Eliot, who with his Chelsea High School curriculum of 1885 sought to develop what he called (and we now call) "power": mental ability to assess reality. Although Eliot's theory of learning was distorted by now discredited views of "faculty psychology"—one studies a subject to exercise certain "muscles" in the mind—his objective was sound. Eliot the chemist employed a mode of analysis that agreed well with Bestor's notion of academic excellence. (Eliot the academic politician, it should be noted, used a brusquer, surer sort of analysis in ruling Harvard.) However, Eliot, Bestor, and other critics of the fifties, such as John T. Latimer, leaped quickly to the current disciplines of language, mathematics, science, and history—the "main-line subjects," as Eliot has termed them. These flourished with new self-confidence in the indulgent fifties—and alas, as then practiced in university after university, were sadly distorted.

The prevailing notion was that of coverage. An English major "covered" the centuries; for each there was an official literature—Beowulf, Chaucer, Spenser, Pope, Milton, Wordsworth, T.S. Eliot. An educated man must be able to recite the first fourteen lines of the *Canterbury Tales* in Middle English. The "what" in a given field dominated, even in the most prestigious universities. Scholars passed on the products of inquiry, not its tools. A doctoral candidate, the budding scholar himself, had to master virtually all the official definitions in a field before exploring its inner workings and scientific process. The fledgling historian, for example, pitted Turner's thesis against Potter's; rarely was he asked to delve into Turner's or Potter's mode of analysis or form of inquiry.

As the "what," the official substance of a subject, dominated, the distinctions between subjects were relatively easily to draw. Milton was English. Cromwell was History. People such as Jefferson or S.F.B. Morse confused things: Jefferson was History, but he was also Political Science, and Art, too. Morse was History, rarely (alas) Art. Hogarth was Art; History suffered from his absence. But, by and large, the corpus of a field could be generally outlined—and was, in endless conferences during the Eisenhower years.

Conferences led by prominent academics gave parameters to the subjects and legitimized them. Insofar as the subjects involved the coverage of mere facts, they made little contribution to *power*, to intellectual discrimination. The conferences were renowned and applauded, heaven knows; but they failed to meet the fundamental intellectual aim that Bestor, Eliot, and others saw as their primary responsibility. The wasteland of sloppy schooling was to be replaced by a wasteland of officially sanctioned but largely inert facts. Gradgrind had found powerful friends.

And so the high schools got Subjects. James Conant unwittingly added to the distortion by creating what he termed an ideal "Academic Inventory," which could be matched with the local high-school curriculum. Conant's inventory was a list of subjects, just as Eliot's had been, and it was just as open to distortion as Eliot's. Frantic and highly criticized schoolmen gave new prominence to the main-line academic subjects and tried to improve their schools' coverage of the official curriculum. Intellectual power was supposedly the goal, but facts predominated.

Rickover's contribution was to focus on American scientific illiteracy. Where Bestor had found young college students naive and without powers of discrimination, Rickover found young men incompetent as engineers and ill-informed as scientists—in a nation self-consciously competing with the Soviet Union. His extended testimony to the Congress highlighted concern over a national weakness in science education, and the National Science Foundation launched two of its earliest projects: a program of curriculum reform, and a study of Soviet scientific and technical manpower, including its training.

The emphasis on content rather than the internal logic of subjects, however laudable, was a distortion. A correction necessarily involved a change in the subjects as scholars defined them, and changes in the university and its myriad departments. The reaction came first in the sciences in the sixties, a period for them of great progress. Revolutionary advances blurred the classical lines of demarcation between subjects within the sciences and favored new modes of inquiry as well. Chemistry, biology, physics, and mathematics often had to merge in practice and be regrouped. The universities, conservative bastions, reacted by adding new subjects: politically self-contained departments of biochemistry, molecular biology, biophysics, applied mathematics. In the same period the social sciences saw few new approaches and little new knowledge, as scholarship there was far from lively. And the humanities slept, and still sleep.

These developments affected the schools, of course. Two figures predominate: Jerrold Zacharias and Jerome Bruner. Zacharias, with the brief collaboration of Francis Friedman, combined the prestige of an M.I.T. professorship and the reputation of an expert on radar and the atomic clock with a concern for teaching the "why" of physics as well as the "what." With the help of James Killian, Zacharias formed the Physical Science Study Committee and established a course in the "new" physics, combining current scholarship with a deliberate emphasis on analysis and process. The course did accept physics as a subject within a defined area of the school timetable and restricted to a certain segment of the school population: in that important sense was it a limited reform. But it represented an attempt at something new—new in approach as well as substance. It was not simply an extension of accepted collegiate practice. Indeed, with its process orientation, its use of several pedagogical media, and its effort at teacher training, PSSC was a marked step beyond conventional college teaching. And Zacharias and the PSSC were not alone. Professional biologists developed three, parallel high-school courses, each emphasizing a different approach, though using much of the same content. This effort reflected the growing interest in process. Similar moves were made in chemistry and mathematics, too. The scientific community, spurred as well as financed by the National Science Foundation, went beyond the Bestor-Conant criticisms to create academically respectable and pedagogically interesting new programs, albeit to fit into unchanged schools in the hierarchy and time frame conventionally provided for the accepted subjects.

The reforms perceived necessary by Bestor and the others were principally directed at high-school-age children and involved intellectual and academic training exclusively. This is no surprise: these critic-reformers were virtually all college men and were dealing day-to-day not with average American youth but with academically inclined students. Although large-scale reforms in the nonacademic areas have yet to be attempted, several groups have addressed themselves to the weak substance in elementary schools. Rudolph Flesch created a stir in the early 1950's with his exposé, *Why Johnny Can't Read*, but no vigorous efforts at reorganization followed: Reading wasn't a subject in the university lexicon, and an alliance between teachers and scholars in linguistics, psychology, and literature was, politically and practically, unthinkable. However, there were some efforts at reform in elementary schools in accepted subjects, particularly in mathematics, the foreign languages, and the sciences. The concern for the approach, or process, was most marked in the sciences. Both the Elementary Science Study (ESS) program developed under Zacharias' guidance at his Educational Services, Inc., and the programs devised under the aegis of the American Association for the Advancement of Science concentrate heavily on scientific process and scientific inquiry. David Hawkins, a key figure in the ESS, even uses the phrase "messing around in science."[3] Such an emphasis on process must give the Arthur Bestor of the 1950's pause!

However, the major stimulus to the interest in process came from Jerome Bruner's *The Process of Education*, an elegant essay that resulted from a scholarly conference on learning. Bruner maintains that knowledge has structure and that that structure can be taught to children. The structure of a subject, Bruner states, is its essence: with this in hand, a person can understand and utilize the subjects in endless ways. To use a mechanical analogy, Bruner wants children to know how and why engines work as well as to attempt to make one work. Memorizing which pieces go on a particular engine in which order does not build "power": that knowledge cannot be applied to another of the endless variety of engines.

Bruner has put his theory to practice in a remarkable social-studies program for ten-year-olds, *Man: A Course of Study*. He chose the most complicated and the most important "engine," man himself, and has sought to bring youngsters to an understanding of how man, among men, lives, grows, and dies. The course puts a series of problems to children, drawing on a variety of human cultures, the explanations and solutions of which provide the beginning of an understanding of the structure of the human individual and his social behavior. Bruner, like Zacharias, used a wide range of elegant and clever materials—superb anthropological films and various kinds of games, for example—and the result is not only an interesting effort at teaching structure but an artistic triumph.

To distort their views somewhat, where Bestor made the

3. David Hawkins, "Messing around in Science," *Science and Children*, vol. 2, no. 5 (February 1965), p. 5.

point that Americans did not *know* enough, Bruner emphasized that they could not *do* enough, in a cognitive sense.
Both, however, were concerned with intellectual *power*: the
ability of an individual accurately to assess reality, to understand it, and to turn it to deliberate uses. A person should
know facts, yes; but important facts; and he should know
how to use them and how to find or create new facts.
Intellectual power has long been part of the rhetorical aims
of American education. Now Zacharias, Bruner, and others
have given new meaning to Whitehead's definition, "the
acquisition of the art of the utilization of knowledge." And
what they advocate is not, in most instances, hostile to the
expectations of Americans regarding intellectual training. The
attempt to sharpen the purposes and the content of academic
training in the schools was not only desirable but politically
feasible.

This is not to say that current efforts at reform are without
blemish. Much too much is still made of "subjects." As *Man:
A Course of Study* demonstrates, children should not necessarily follow the same categories that scholars use in organizing knowledge. The Bruner course is a careful blending of
history, anthropology, economics, politics, sociology, and
more. That it is a mix does not mean that it is sloppy, or
intellectually indefensible. The critics of the fifties were
scathing about the vapidity of the social-studies programs in
schools, but they incorrectly diagnosed the trouble as an
unwholesome amalgam of disciplines rather than sloppy
scholarship. Few scholars have had the audacity (and vision)
to cross subject lines, as Bruner did, with both impunity and
intellectual respectability. More like him are needed, particularly to concentrate on other key areas of power, such as
reading and simple logic. The humanities, too, cry out for
reform. Yet, curiously, scholars in the humanities and arts
seem unable to surge forth with the imagination and courage
displayed by the scientists. University scholarship in these
areas is itself sterile; as long as this is so, there is little chance

for serious reforms on behalf of children. What's more, the vacuum is being filled increasingly by so-called humanistic psychologists, many of whom are as ignorant of the arts as humanistic scholars are of the need for change. One has nightmares that humanistic education in the schools will become one, undisciplined, narcissistic T-group.

In addition, the university-oriented Bestor group—if one can call it that—is uncertain what effect social class differences and the child's total environment will have on learning. The most elegant work done by them is for use in accepted subjects in traditional schools for children like the scholars' own children. This is not to say that the curricula developed cannot be effective with low-income (or high-income) children, only that that potential is still largely untried. Schoolmen working in slums have found the new curricula only marginally helpful, however. All too few children there reach the point where a physics course, for example, is even a possibility. Moreover, the cultural "baggage" that different groups of children bring to school has to be dealt with and capitalized upon. Current curriculum reform tends to assume that it will be middle-class baggage. And all too few movements look to the effect of the entire school day on a child. The courses address a fraction of the school day; few broad, multidiscipline efforts aimed at a variety of approaches to power have emerged.

The journals are full of the call by educators and scholars for efforts of this kind. But no group, except an underfunded school here or there, has attempted an experiment on a sustained, massive scale. The United States government has spent over $20 million to reform high-school physics in the last ten years, and its effect is yet being challenged as superficial. What if proportionally higher sums could be spent on a more comprehensive effort? The problem is not that money could not be coaxed out of Washington but that leadership is lacking. The reformers have been either critics (they cursed or prescribed, but did not create) or inventors

tied to their university subject and loath to leave it. True
power is a Renaissance thing: we want children to have
intellectual skills that range across organized knowledge. But
we elders lack the courage to range across it ourselves in the
interest of children. As a result, nothing will happen. Or the
gap will be filled, willy-nilly, by Bestor's nemesis, the nonintellectual "educationist."

Power, as the word has been used here so far, means
intellectual power. This meaning is in keeping with conventional expectations and aims such as Whitehead's. There are
other kinds of power, of course, notably manual and kinetic.
A child should know how to do something with his hands as
well as his mind: our culture will never be one of brains
alone. Indeed, it is not possible to understand some problems
fully without the recognition of the constraints imposed by
physical reality. One sees more in a Rembrandt portrait after
one has tried oneself to work with oil, brush, and canvas.
Careful work with laboratory balances gives new significance
to the precise properties of solids. But the disciplines of hand
and eye do not simply support the mind: they have a life of
their own and give power by opening the way to new kinds
of expression and understanding. The average American
rarely understands these potentials, and neither does his local
school authority. Their view of nonintellectual power depends on "usefulness": manual skills, from those of plumber
to those of surgeon, are economically employable. It seems
reasonable to expect education to provide these skills, so
necessary if at any time the individual is attracted by a career
that requires manual dexterity. Moreover, a clever educator
can bootleg the more profound uses of manual power within
this framework and within conventionally described academic courses as well. Kinetic power, however—the use of the
body—is completely foreign to American educators and
almost impossible to bootleg within one of the standard
subjects. The English have done interesting work in what
they call "movement" in primary schools and seemingly are

giving youngsters a sense of control over their bodies and a sense of their capacity for expressiveness. The more utilitarian American sees the mind and hand as producers, not as means of expression. As a result, our children are denied a form of communication and a sense of control.

Intellectual power, with subsidiary emphasis on manual power, remains the most persistent general aim of American education. However, the glib academic critic today denigrates it (just as in the early fifties the critics exalted and thus distorted it). Particularly when prescribing for the "disadvantaged," too many critics have recommended programs largely devoted to self-awareness, group pride, and expression. Tough intellectual demands are often nonexistent; and academic content is to be added only when a child begins to "know himself" and "have confidence." Such thinking is as dangerous as it is careless. How can anyone truly know himself without the kind of structure and background represented in the learning of *Man: A Course of Study* or its equivalent? And what better kind of confidence is there than that which results from mastering the power that the culture prizes and rewards most highly? More important, power, particularly intellectual power, is the essence of economic, political, and cultural advance, whether for the individual or for the group. People who are incapable of sharp analysis, who are unable to see a situation whole or to use knowledge are easily subjugated—as the American black ruefully knows. Those who comfortably mock the importance of rigorous intellectual training should look carefully at Kenneth Clark's supposedly radical plan for the Washington, D.C., public schools to concentrate massively on reading and language skills. Clark is saying that *power*, the intellectual skills that give individuals a range of possibilities, is of central importance: hardly a radical notion. He would not bombard his children with propaganda (and, now that the Washington schools are almost totally Negro, they are, racially, Clark's children); he would give them skills. Those of either race who

would start with a child's attitudes and emotions and nothing
else do the youngster a disservice. Power comes first, or at
least is concurrent with feeling and style. And intellectual
power is of primary importance for those against whom
society discriminates. It is the key weapon with which to
strike back in a lasting, effective way.

Americans, of course, have wanted more from their schools
than power alone. They expect education to give children
"culture"—to teach each child what his place in society is and
what society demands of him. This can be called a sense of
agency: the personal style, assurance, and self-control that
allow an individual to act in both socially acceptable and
personally meaningful ways. Agency has two aspects, and
they are often in conflict, though the conflict is almost
always glossed over in American rhetoric. On one side stands
the individual: education should help him to "find" himself,
to become an autonomous, self-controlled, unique person.
On the other stands corporate society: education should be
its agent to assure that the young understand the demands
and responsibilities that the culture imposes. Purveyors of
conventional rhetoric ignore the conflict: of course the
red-blooded American boy will decide on his own to accept
and safeguard the existing demands and responsibilities of the
society! The more perceptive see the dilemma and generally
arrange for society to win. No nation (it is supposed) can
afford *truly* autonomous youth; even Jefferson understood
that. Individualism, then, is prominent in the rhetoric, but
societal responsibilities (or, put in the pejorative, conformity)
remain paramount both in practice and in the expectations of
adult citizens.

The most obvious clash between individual and corporate
needs comes with employability. The youth needs to have
marketable skills, confidence to use them effectively, a capacity to learn new skills, and a sense of what is right for him,
what he will *like* doing. He needs, in sum, competence,

confidence, and pride. Society, on the other hand, needs people skilled to perform corporately required tasks in a dependable, accurate manner. One hopes that individual skills and desires will mesh with the requirements of the labor market, but they do not always. So, moreover, those responsible for corporate development emphasize current skills over a competence to learn new skills (despite the rhetoric to the contrary), and when considering employees' motivations, their likes, they do not think beyond bonuses, stock options, paid holidays, and Musak. Labor is purely an economic artifact.

This is not surprising and not, as many self-styled radicals would have us believe, of itself immoral. In a world of endless riches, every man could be educated in what interested him for as many years as he desired. There would be no such thing as an "oversupply" of high-school graduates, of B.A.'s or Ph.D.'s: the intrinsic reward of study would be an end unto itself. Education would be entirely a consumer good, an enterprise designed exclusively for individual gratification and development toward personal ends. But our resources are not endless, and people with certain kinds of skills may be needed at a given point in time more than others; the state then encourages them by supporting them handsomely, at the expense of others. It sees education, at least in part, as production, the vehicle to create skills which themselves forward the economy in desirable ways.

Several problems emerge here. First, men are not happy in any important psychological and personal sense unless they are *needed*, honestly desired by some respected social group for some end. The elegantly schooled but unemployed person quickly sees himself as a parasite and rarely respects himself for long. Thus, people want to prepare themselves for what is wanted by the society; an educational system planned systematically on labor-market projections provides, roughly, what individuals in fact desire. They desire to be "in demand." If engineers are needed, and, accordingly, honored in every way society can honor, then people will happily become engineers and will *like* being engineers.

The rub comes in the manner in which labor-market projections are made. What one man may need, another man may find extraneous. The labor market is, of course, just one (albeit important) part of a social plan based on social objectives, objectives which are normative and highly debatable. Furthermore, planners make mistakes (or ignore the implications of their own projections); planning is hardly an exact science. Equally important is the gap between a desirable plan and social traditions. A planner may find that more nurses and primary-school teachers are needed, but society as a whole may not be ready at that moment to reward those occupations. There are many important jobs that lack the status they deserve, and few people want a job without status. Thus, a conflict exists not just between the wishes of the individual and the needs of corporate society, but also between corporate needs and social value systems.

Since World War II, educational reform has been increasingly influenced by the ideas of "human resource" planners. Much of their early work related to the allocation of resources to formal education in poor, newly independent countries in Africa, Latin America, and Asia. Their recommendations for these nations drew on exploratory work carried out over the past thirty years by scholars such as Theodore Shultz, Frederick Harbison, Fritz Machlup, Charles Myers, and the political scientist James Coleman, who have studied the impact of formal schooling on economic and political development. These men sought to assess the effect schooling has on society as a whole. They were able to identify few specific results, but they found evidence of what might be called a residual factor: after all else had been taken into account, the measured politico-economic growth (or decline) appeared to be correlated with educational investment (or lack thereof).

Except on a very general level, then, current social-science scholarship gives us only limited direction. We can calculate, as Fritz Machlup has done, the economic "costs" of keeping mothers and young people out of the labor market—not "producing"—and we can envision model simulations of what might happen if we did not. We can show that economic growth of certain kinds requires a labor force with a particular percentage of workers having specialized intellectual and vocational skills. An economic unit which does not have these skills at its disposal (either by creating its own or by using others') cannot achieve the desired growth. Political scientists may urge a balance between advanced education for the elite, which is essential for economic advance, and politically popular mass primary education. If a country directs all its resources toward schooling for children, it will not be able to provide technical colleges and universities, and vice versa. The trick is to hit on an economically sound formula which is politically feasible.

The concept of educational planning is relatively new. Asserting aims and goals is as old as man himself, but creating and using sophisticated tools to assess current and future effects of formal education is a modern phenomenon. It has increasingly influenced the way people think about education. As mentioned earlier, nineteenth-century schooling was expected to cover the rudiments and to provide symbols of status. Training toward production (vocational training, broadly defined) was to be had on the job. In recent years, this notion has been altered: increasingly, the schools are justified primarily as producers, as purveyors of the intellectual and vocational wealth that is part of a general plan for social advance. An institution of formal education is accountable for this production; it has to meet its projected output.

This revised view of the purpose of schools is part of the current high expectations for education. Given the state of the art of planning, however, it gives rise to several problems. Many people still believe that schools should help the individual first and society second, inasmuch as a powerful, autonomous individual is the basis of a truly free society. But economists have not been able to calculate the output such anarchically educated individuals will provide; indeed, such individuals may simply become troublemakers, in every sense. Furthermore, as Benjamin Franklin reminded us two hundred years ago, art is long and time is short; there is much knowledge and far less time to learn it all. One must learn what is socially most important and most useful.

Americans are increasingly skeptical both of what has been called "general" education and of a system of specialization that depends wholly on individual choice. We hear much of "waste" and "overproduction" of graduates in this or that field. These judgments are all in terms of society: we waste money by providing education that does not, now or in the future, produce. That it may be personally enriching (and wholly unrelated to any economic or political end) is irrelevant.

A sense of agency, then, emerges from how and why a person is needed. Is he employable? If he isn't, he suffers physically and psychologically. Does he have skills that give him confidence, a sense of what is personally possible for him, a sense of his worth as a contributor to society? If he doesn't, he flounders. An individual's own sense of worth is subtly tied to the social order. The radical may say that the individual should be committed to altering the existing order; a conservative may say that he should be equipped to forward it, to produce for it. Both assert that there must be some accommodation, some understanding by an individual of his place, of his worth, in the social and economic order. Lenin knew his worth; so did Henry Ford.

Recently, this point has been taken a step further, notably by the sociologist James Coleman. The effectiveness of education, in both personal and corporate terms, it is hypothesized, is a function of the close interaction of formal education and the economy. An individual develops most productively when he sees the purpose of his study. It is not just abstract; it is connected to life, to action. The more lifelike the setting of the problems he is studying, the more effectively and profoundly he learns. This doctrine is hardly new, of course: it is a cornerstone of John Dewey's view that formal education is fundamentally learning from life, and that the school should, as far as possible, become a microcosm of life; and it is at the heart of current school practice in Maoist China. The motiviation of a student largely depends, then, on the closeness of the connection between the abstract learning expected of him and the "real world." Coleman and others extend this by suggesting that an individual needs to be self-evidently *productive* in a social or economic sense, as well as in an individual sense, as a condition for learning. He must be doing something important and constructive which has an end other than his own intellectual and social development, something that adds directly to the community. A school, as it were, should be a factory, having a primary output of some kind of goods and only a secondary output of educated youth. We have long heard of adding schools to factories. Now we have factories added to schools, not just to help the latter balance their budgets (a tactic tried with little success by many nineteenth-century academies and colleges), but to add a sense of extrinsic worth as the basis for the education of children.[4]

Variations of this theme abounded in the Progressive era. The work terms at Bennington, Antioch, and elsewhere, and the work-study system practiced at Northeastern University are attempts to let life itself teach. Most secondary schools and colleges have social-service activities that put youngsters in the real world. But Bennington put a student into an on-going enterprise primarily to learn from it, not to become a producer within it. The learner was a visitor, not a long-term, committed participant. And social-service activities were often motivated by feelings of guilt, by *noblesse*

4. Coleman's thesis was presented informally at a conference at Ditchley Park, Oxfordshire [U.K.], in February 1971. On China, see, for example, Andrew Watson's article in the London *Times* of 15 May 1971, "Acoustics of a Closed Society."

oblige, the favored lending a brief (and often arrogant) hand
to the destitute. The services provided help for the poor and
salved the consciences of the rich. They were not to give the
student a sense of worth, of action, of productivity in any
central sense; they were add-ons, *extra*curricular.

There is something fanciful in the idea of making youngsters truly active producers, in having their abstract education
build on a continuing experience as producers. Few smaller
children could ever be producers, except in the Dickensian
sense. It is difficult, too, to imagine employers in a capitalist
society today risking profits on the output of children, or
labor unions allowing public-school-factories to operate. Pris-
on workshops are barely tolerated as competitors to private
industry: who can seriously imagine that schools, which are
far more numerous, would be welcome? However unfeasible,
these suggestions for reform underscore the sensible, but too
often ignored, point that a sense of worth—an individual
sense of one's own importance and one's own power—
emerges from successful participation in life itself. Exclusively vicarious experience is risky. The dreamer is frightened
when he awakes, however bold he is while asleep. The active
participant, perhaps not so bold in the light of day, develops
real confidence and a true sense of pride. Conversely, the
more abstract and unconnected formal education is to economic society, the less it will provide a basis for personal
confidence, psychological security, and pride. The winner of
prizes at all too many existing schools is insecure in life: the
prizes have nothing to do with a grasp over life. The little boy
who is a successful entrepreneur—one of those whom Mary
Engel has called "Saturday's children," small youngsters who
work regularly and successfully for pay in addition to
attending school or playing hookey—has a sense of worth
that is obvious to the most casual observer. (That sense can
be knocked out of him, too, Mrs. Engel found.)[5]

5. Mary Engel, "Saturday's Children: A Study of Working Boys," *Harvard
Studies in Career Development* 33 (September 1964).

In brief, the individual's right to a sense of worth, and to a vocation which he likes, and the society's right to organize its own development by subtly (or not so subtly) assigning individuals to jobs are only partly in contradiction. The existing economy profoundly affects an individual's sense of personal worth. "Making it" confers pride, a sense of achievement, a sense of agency. "Making it" means mastering the economy and society as they are, accepting most of their values and constraints, and working effectively within them. And "making it" has been a rhetorical aim of education and an expectation of most Americans for generations. (Of course, those who control, and plan, the labor market can thereby gain an insidious hold on the population's motivations. Clever dictators have made much of this.)

A sense of worth, however, depends on more than economic involvement. Feelings of personal importance, of uniqueness, of confidence, have a psychological basis related to but also functionally irrelevant to a productive career. The need for these feelings is innately human; their achievement does not come by chance but, like most important attitudes, develops through the contexts in which people find themselves. These contexts can be arranged, at least up to a point, and one might expect society to see that happy contexts exist, even when they are unrelated or only partially related to economic productivity.

The sad fact is that this end—the sense of uniqueness and self-importance for individuals rather than in the interest of corporate aims—is ignored in practice (if not in rhetoric). Moreover, educators have created contexts which are themselves destructive. Is a person aware of his uniqueness and worth when he is only a name on a list, one in some category or other? Are pride and confidence fostered by sarcasm, or by the denigration of one's individual values? Is a sense of power developed if one is given no responsibility, if one is forced to live knowing that no adult trusts him? Of course not. But too many schools operate this way, unconsciously or because they have no alternative. In this sense, it is not hyperbole to say that some schools "destroy the hearts and minds of children," as Jonathan Kozol has put it. Children, even adolescents, are treated in categories: "the Room 314 eleventh-grade group." They are assigned by categories, "tracked" or "streamed" on the basis of apparent academic talents—rarely on the basis of individual wishes or a personal need for challenge and reward. (The effects of this pigeon-holing attitude of teachers have been devastatingly exposed by Robert Rosenthal and Leonore Jacobsen in *Pygmalion in the Classroom:* it appears that children succeed who are *supposed* to by virtue of tests, even when the test results have been secretly juggled. Children who are expected by the teacher to score high, or low, do so, irrespective of their real talents.) A child is not John Smith, Unique Person; a child is a Third-Grader, Robin Group; or a Commercial-Track Senior. The child who does not conform to the way adults have organized school is summarily punished. Rarely are his reasons for rebellion considered, or accommodated. School is a place to learn Adult Things, and adults decide what those Things are and how they are to be learned. The child's view is worthless; reward comes only when the child borrows adult views and puts them into practice. Adults are Quiet and Don't Squirm and Like to Learn about Czechoslovakia (or pretend to). If you want rewards, or to avoid being yelled at, Be Quiet, Don't Squirm, and Be Interested in Bohemians (the geographical kind, which is the only kind that exists for school). In other words, my child, don't be a child. If you want to be a Good Adult someday, start acting like one now.

America values its traditional heroes—and we all know who they are. It would be unthinkable for a child to find Lincoln a skillful but rather unpleasant opportunist, or Washington a stuffy aristocratic slave owner, or Franklin a dirty old man. History tells us that Aaron Burr was entirely in the wrong. Nathan Hale was a good spy; Major André was a bad spy. The Boston Massacre was bad; the repression of Aguinaldo and the Philippine people was just. America always progresses, and gets better all the time: we should be grateful, and patient. The Negro child who finds George Washington's slaveholding hardly laudable and W.E.B. DuBois's courage ennobling is wrong, and is taught so by implication if not explicitly. Robert Frost's country poems may seem less meaningful to some than the city poems of Langston Hughes, but the child is expected to appreciate Frost because he is a Great Poet. And who (until very recently) ever heard of Hughes? Obviously there is no one pantheon of heroes, no one set of great poets, no immutable application of justice, no one reading of history for all individuals, and to the extent that schools teach single values and views, some children suffer severely. And most schools do teach from a single point of view; and some children, as a result, find school hardly fulfilling; in fact, destructive. It is not simply that their children's opinions and ideas are not rewarded: far from it. Opinions and ideas must be challenged and defended and, in the light of new insight, altered. It is that their views are not even considered, not respected in any form at all.

The child, even the sixteen-year-old, is taught to Be Responsible, but only in the abstract: if he wishes to go to the "basement" (a euphemism for toilet), he needs a pass. Children are told what drill they require to master a skill, and rarely asked what drill they themselves feel they might need. The general assumption in school is that the child needs to be protected from himself—while learning how to Get Along in Life.

The foregoing examples may be an exaggeration in the case of some schools and classrooms, but not in most. Most schools are monuments of contradiction—teaching the virtues of tolerance while insisting on an imposed party line; teaching self-respect while not respecting children; teaching the necessities of citizenship while ignoring the most elemental graces of civility. They teach about the delicacies of cleanliness but maintain washrooms of insensitive squalor. They preach individualism but teach by platoons. Such is the reality of schools, and so has it been for decades, the rhetoric notwithstanding. It is adults' most tragic lie to children.

In recent years, this lie has provoked a literature of rage, a gaggle of angry, and often inspired, books describing how schools stunt and cheat children. The thread that runs through all this writing is the belief that children should be allowed to find themselves, should be allowed to develop a feeling of worth by being respected for what they are, should grow as children, not as sawed-off adults, should glory in the best values of their group rather than solely in majoritarian American values. Above all, children must be *respected*, as individuals as important and as precious as any adult of whatever renown. Schools should respect children because they are children: this, it is argued, is elementary civility. A happy result of such respect (but not the primary reason for it, it must be stressed) is the emergence of a creative context for development. Children find self-respect in a setting which honors them. And, with a feeling of pride and confidence, they learn well and deeply. A moral context, happily, becomes an intellectually creative context.

Fortunately, many of these angry books have had wide readership, at least as wide as books on education ever have. Some temper their rage with humor, none with more delightful malice than Bel Kaufman in *Up the Down Staircase.* Kozol's *Death at an Early Age*, Jim Haskins' *Diary of a Harlem Schoolteacher*, parts of Claude Brown's *Manchild in a Promised Land* and John Holt's *How Children Fail*, among others, are chronicles, each with its own tale. Other writers highlight the horror by focusing on alternative situations: Nat Hentoff's description of Elliott Shapiro's lively slum school *(Our Children are Dying)*, James Herndon's account of his own efforts with poor youngsters *(The Way It Spozed to Be)*, or Herbert Kohl's of his work *(Thirty-Six Children)*. The teacher-writers of this genre form a cohesive, lively group, and cynics point out how often they are asked to write (predictably laudatory) reviews of each other's books. They have few apparent gurus, save perhaps New Zealand's Sylvia Ashton-Warner (whose attitude of respect toward the particularly rambunctious Maori children is legendary), Paul Goodman, and the English exponents of the "free day" and "open" primary schools. Their academic roots reach to Froebel, Piaget, Dewey, and Bruner. Their political allies are, not surprisingly, some of the less militant leaders of oppressed minority groups. Their emphasis on respect and cultural diversity is in marked contrast to the practices of public schools available to most black, Puerto Rican, Indian, and Chicano youngsters. Young teachers usually respond to their views, particularly before they get used to the system.

This group has been called radical but is so only in that its members find the existing educational apparatus inconsistent with human dignity and civil rights. Their positive views are hardly radical, being staples of long-approved American social rhetoric: honor and respect of others, cultural diversity, and justice. Telling an emperor that he has no clothes on may appear radical to the emperor, but it is mere reasonable honesty to the less involved observer.

These critics have also been called "romantics," usually in a pejorative sense. They are romantic in the way that Rousseau and Froebel are romantic. They believe in the innate goodness of children and in the happy effects of freedom. No Calvinist original sin here; they, very simply, believe that children are good and that helping them grow up in a loving, respectful manner will allow them to become self-confident, worthwhile people. Some of these critics are indeed impractical, or even irresponsible; they identify the evils but give no realistic suggestions for correcting them. Changing the attitude of all teachers, or shutting down all public schools, or abolishing all administrative posts hardly qualifies as a useful first, or even second, step in a reform program. Even worse is the cop-out on the part of some of these writers. The society is hopeless, they say, so let us retreat with our own kind and do our thing in isolation. Put off by scornful rhetoric, many public school educators have dismissed the ideas of these critics wholesale—ideas which in fact have sprung from a long, American, philosophical tradition and from a historic concept of the nature of children.

The views of these so-called romantic critics are consistent with recent trends in the psychological and anthropological study of children. Piaget's developmental approach and his assertion that childhood is a stage, or rather a series of stages, in life has gained advocates in academia; recent work along these lines at Harvard, Chicago, and elsewhere is highly promising. Lawrence Kohlberg's work on the stages of moral development sheds new light not only on how children shape their values but also on how a school might help youngsters to be morally more discriminating. Gerald Lesser's comparative studies of the mental abilities of children from differing racial and cultural groups point up important differences in style and form (while inevitably agitating those who fear comparisons and giving fuel, also, to bigots)—differences which deserve to be considered and accommodated in schools. This work, too, reinforces the intuitive feelings of teachers who believe their task is to help youngsters move with increasing autonomy through a series of steps of increasing complexity and sophistication. These teachers do not think they are there to provide models of maturity against which a child is periodically measured. Children aren't small adults but children.

These sophisticated approaches to education notwithstanding, there are clear reasons why the schools remain as they are, not geared to honor the state of childhood and not organized to respect individuality and diversity. Most Americans have very generalized notions about heroes and conduct. The schools are expected to impose these. Minority views are a threat, so they are played down. The rhetoric calls for diversity, but what is expected is majority values, crisply and inexpensively taught, and that is what results. Pluralism is acceptable in speeches, but—quite understandably—not in practice. And *individual* agency, a feeling of worth, self-respect, and self-confidence, is not considered as important as the sense of agency that assists production in the economy. The society clearly benefits from the latter, and, not surprisingly, supports it. The former is nice, but expendable. Everyone wants teachers to respect children, of course, to nurture them and make allowances for their individuality—as long as it doesn't cost anything. Unfortunately, a policy of pluralism can be expensive, both in time and in terms of human energy. Platoons of children can be managed with a handful of teachers. The accommodation of individual idiosyncrasies would require more adults, or adults with special skills and sensitivity. Idiosyncrasies call for new books and apparatus, for trips here and there, for the breaking of taboos and traditions. They might lead to a policy permitting some children to spend extended periods out of school, on jobs, or at home.

Compulsory school attendance, in practice, has meant just that: attendance at school. But if the requirement were, sensibly, reconstituted to mean "compulsory educational involvement," one might find youngsters participating in learning in all kinds of settings, including schools as we know them. Even in outline, this approach (which will be considered in detail in a later chapter) conflicts with the expectation of most Americans that kids will stay in school until they are sixteen, out from under Mom's feet and not in competition for Dad's job. The idea of varied settings and flexible timing for formal education may be logical, but it will have a hard time coming into practice. Accommodation to individual desires and special needs is painful, and it is expensive. And in terms of accountability, it doesn't make an explicit, immediately visible contribution to society.

Respect requires civil surroundings and endless patience, which would require many resources, both fiscal and human. These are not forthcoming. Schools are financed as mass institutions, operated for maximum efficiency on a platoon system with a minimum of amenities. The sensitive school-man, though he might agree with Holt, Kozol, Kaufman, and the others, is in large measure trapped. What he considers important for children is not what the local leaders consider important; his values do not square with the community's expectations. He is caught between the constraints of the system—public expectations and public support—and the lash of the critics. With teachers cursed from both quarters, the profession becomes a particularly trying one.

A final aspect of a sense of agency deserves special emphasis. A reasonable aim of education is that schools help individuals develop a personal set of values. An equally reasonable aim of education is that schools pass along to youngsters the values of the society, the codes by which the community lives. An individual's values, responsibly arrived at, might, however, be at odds with the community's values, which may be responsible unto themselves. An accommodation is then required. Neither extreme is exactly attractive: a community of Thoreaus would be anarchic; a community of social sycophants would be tyrannic.

Society requires individuals who have self-control, who are prepared to accept verdicts arrived at by democratic process, who are tolerant of honest differences, respect person and property, are civil (at least in public), and who accept responsibility when duty calls. Traditionally, society expects schools to inculcate these traits and values. This is society's stake in fostering a sense of agency: the need for personally motivated, thoughtful citizens. Society needs people whose instincts support the common weal, individuals who, at their best, lead the democracy or, at their least, unobtrusively and lawfully fit in.

It can be argued, on the other hand, that an individual has a right to his *own* values, and that neither schools nor any other social agency should attempt to mold them. This argument is foolish, of course: no man's values are ever solely individualistic, sprung pure from an unobligated mind. The culture presses on the most resistant individualist, and a man's freedom from it is only a matter of degree. Even within these constraints, however, there are serious problems. Does a man have the right to be a bigot? Surely yes, unless he inflicts that bigotry on others, at which point society must restrain him. No community that tolerates bigotry is healthy (as Americans know all too well). A community restricts individual *actions*, actions that, while springing from personal convictions, threaten social stability. To that extent, no man is wholly free.

Schools should teach the limits of both personal rights and corporate rights. The interstices between them are for the courts to adjudicate, but both the individual and the community must agree upon a code of justice and a system of due process to settle differences. These are complex matters—far beyond the scope of these essays—but profoundly important for education. The schools should help children develop an autonomous set of values and should make children familiar through history, philosophy, and literature with the traditions and problems that men have faced through the ages and still face. The schools should also teach the norms of the society. Presumably, too, they should be prepared to cope with the clash between the two. Should schools, then, teach a concept of justice that provides a framework for accommodation, a fair system for choosing between conflicting claims? If they do so, the schools themselves are taking a moral position. If they don't, they are sidestepping the most agonizing question children must grapple with.

In practice, of course, current rhetoric is full of contradictions. The leaders tell us that every child develops his own ideas and that there is no single position taken in a school on any question of values. Religion, they say, is absent, as the law stipulates. A wall of separation exists, or so we hear. Most Americans accept this as so—and expect the majority values to be quietly imposed. Conventional American norms are, for many, simply not debatable; they are fixed verities, above discussion and obvious for all. The school should teach these, without question.

General expectations notwithstanding, there is no such thing as a value-free school. Schools have to take moral positions just to operate. They have to treat children in one way or another and thus willy-nilly teach a set of norms by example. No teacher exists in a vacuum, wholly value-free (how dull he would be!), nor is any teacher conceivably able to argue every side of every issue. He selects and in so doing implies values. The very act of presenting several sides of an issue is itself an expression of a value. As for religion, however defined, it is inevitably "taught" in countless classrooms. One cannot discuss history, literature, or the arts, without some consideration of church doctrine and of peoples' religious motivations. Formal religion is on many children's minds; and no good teacher can avoid, eventually, what is on the children's minds.

And so the schools preach that they are essentially value-free, respecting all viewpoints and excluding religion. In fact, they are unambiguously expected to teach values, albeit implicitly, if only to function; in addition, they are expected by most Americans to teach majority social norms. The tragedy is that most Americans do not see these norms as debatable issues. For most of us, they are fixed, immutable as the Rocky Mountains. Such naiveté corrupts education.

Fostering a sense of agency is an especially important aim of education for Americans. Personal style—manners, assurance, self-control, proper ambition, something to offer the society that the society needs, patriotism—these are all traditional goals for schools. Individuality in a personal sense is accepted, but honored only in the breach. Reasonable and desirable though this complex purpose of agency is, the attempt to accomplish it is tearing the schools and communities apart, for the community's ends and the individual's are often at odds. If schools were to serve merely as mediators, perhaps they could help. As it is, the conflict is rhetorically sluffed over, and the community's values are enforced. This can scarcely nurture a sense of agency.

The more Calvinist, achievement-oriented Americans would rarely list joy as a goal of education. The concept of joy makes most Americans uncomfortable: it's all right for angels on the occasion of Christ's resurrection or for teenagers after winning a football game—but it really isn't, well, respectable. What's more, the words used to describe joyfulness are hackneyed and saccharine, at best stereotyped, frilly words: awareness, faith, wonder, love, spontaneity, expressiveness, feeling.

Schools have been expected to teach appreciation of beauty, however. Most Americans believe that a child has a right to learn about Art, and a responsibility to develop aesthetic discrimination, or taste. In many schools, though, this means that he is expected to like "good" art and eschew the "bad," to like Beethoven and Winslow Homer and to dislike the Beatles and gasoline-station calendars. This, of course, mocks any real sense of art and art criticism: but mockery, alas, is abroad in our schools and colleges, even in our most distinguished and presumably sophisticated universities.

The right of children to aesthetic experience is reasonable, and, as that experience is rarely gained by chance, the society has a clear responsibility to meet it in some formal manner. Much of art is, of course, power, in the sense we have described. A child has a right to aesthetic power. He also has a right to aesthetic feeling, and this, too, can be developed or, better, provided for. Exposing youngsters to a number of artistically creative settings, giving them various media to work with, extending their vicarious experience of the feelings of artists—all these are pedagogically possible. Every man should have access to the joy of beauty, of shape, sound, color. He should be able to sing inside. The likelihood that he will have that option cannot be left, responsibly, to chance. And the confusion of that end with the learning of official taste deserves to be exposed.

In realms outside the arts, the *absence* of joy has been a concern of schoolmen since the Progressive era. Public concern is usually expressed the other way around: schools should try to keep children from being miserable. The most miserable, to the Progressives, were the emotionally distressed; and spurred both by the teaching of Freud and by associated new perspectives on mental illness, major efforts were made to provide "personal guidance." Gradually, psychological services were provided for all children, not just those who were "ill." In many schools, unfortunately, personal counseling has been primarily concerned with vocational guidance in its narrowest sense. The counselor figuratively asks all in one breath: Who are you? What do you want to be? Do you want me to suggest plumbing firms for you to have interviews with? These three concerns are, for many youngsters, very much in conflict, and few counselors have the time and freedom from administrative chores, much less the competence and sensitivity, to cope with them. The third being the easiest point for the counselor to help with, it is the one most often dealt with. To a considerable degree, moreover, guidance has been primarily focused on the child's sense of agency, as defined earlier, and marginal attention has been paid to the child's happiness or ability to understand and express feeling.

A great deal of emphasis was put, in the 1930's and 1940's, on "adjustment to life." As used, the term encompassed joy as well as agency, and it implied that the American way was a good way, a perfectly adequate way to find happiness and full means of expression. Happiness could best be found in adjustment to the society as it was. Rebellion, for whatever reason, was a sign of misery.

More subtle approaches have been tried in recent times. In many communities where there is agitation involving schools, much is made of the joy (or absence of pain) that comes from a greater awareness of one's personality and that of others around you. Various techniques, most involving group training, are being used. Their purpose is to heighten individual consciousness and in so doing increase sensitivity and reduce hurtful and unconstructive conflict. In education, this group work has largely involved teachers rather than children, and its effectiveness is still being debated. It assumes, as did the life-adjustment approach, that the existing social structures are right (or, if not right, not the principal concern for "training"), and that an eased ("more joyful") situation can come from mild group therapy. It is a remedial, rather than a revolutionary, approach. Most Americans find these efforts at easing pain and conflict desirable, if a bit suspect and peripheral; certainly most find them harmless.

But joy means more than mere absence of pain, or even heightened sensitivity to one's surroundings and to people. It can mean a condition of individual liberty well outside the contexts of a particular social situation. In this sense, joy does not depend on adjustment to a particular setting; it ignores the setting. Joy in this broader sense is affective individualism, a state of personal freedom. It is not hedonistic anarchy, its advocates contend. True self-realization involves selflessness and caring, along with creativity. A compact for social action based on love might replace traditional power politics. In part, this characterization of joy is a form of agency in the sense of knowing who one is within society. In another, it is power, knowing how to use skills for personal ends. This is the "ecstasy" of which George B. Leonard has written, the "delight in learning."[6] But the skills involved are more than traditionally rational tools. Rationality is one way of perceiving reality and deciding on action. Feeling and intuition—nonrational, but not necessarily irrational—are others. A criterion of self-fulfillment, or joy, is a

6. George B. Leonard, *Education and Ecstasy* (New York, 1968).

basis for decision, as objective logic has long been in the best of academe. The *quality* of self-fulfillment is crucial, and there is these days much interest, some serious and some less so, in discovering ways to extend this fulfillment to the limit of the human potential.

This point of view alters in interesting ways the classic dilemma of individual ends versus social requirements. In one sense, it is the quintessence of selfishness: the point of existence is *self*-fulfillment, *self*-actualization, *self*-reward. It is painfully introspective. Yet it carries the promise that the corporate effect of a new morality based on self-realizing joy will inevitably lessen social anguish. Its emphasis is on community, the self-fulfillment of individuals joined to become group fulfillment. The rewards in this system are intrinsic, in how one feels about it—rather than extrinsic, in the status and wealth society bestows. In this respect, it is strikingly Christian, even Franciscan. And it conflicts with the expectations most Americans have for their youth and with what they want their educational institutions to provide. This view of joy is profoundly revolutionary.

The movement's current high priest is Charles A. Reich— incongruously, a guardian of analytic rationality, a professor of law. His paean to the movement, *The Greening of America*, has struck a responsive chord among relatively well-to-do, educated youth. No doubt, it is largely ignored by most Americans; and, incredibly, it overlooks the real aspirations (laudable or not) of less wealthy sectors of the population. Yet it provides a benchmark that educators who must deal with youth from all social classes would be senseless to ignore. Moreover, Reich makes an important ideological link to the philosophy of education expressed in the "literature of rage" of Messrs. Holt, Dennison, Kohl, et al. "All of this search for increased consciousness [by newly awakened youth]," Reich writes, "culminates in an attitude that is the very antithesis of [conventional norms]: a desire for innocence, for the ability to be in a state of wonder or awe. It is of the essence of the thinking of the new generation that man should be constantly open to new experience, constantly ready to have his old ways of thinking changed, constantly hoping that he will be sensitive enough and receptive enough to let the wonders of nature and mankind come to him."[7] In a word, that man be perpetually in a state of *development.* Although these views are now held by only a small minority of Americans, the combination of these with the commitments of the "romantic radicals" by a number of young teachers who are not too proud to use old-style political leverage on existing institutions could have a signal effect on American education.

Power, sense of agency, joy, then: all part of American educational rhetoric. All overlapping and complex. All honored as generalities but bedeviled with contradictions in their specifics. But the educational system runs on generalities, as that is all that those who govern and those who pay for American education care to consider. The rest, to them, is mere detail. The existence of fundamental inconsistencies in our stated goals is dismissed as "just a management problem." And so American education stumbles on, not *mindless* really, but tangled in contradictions it dares not face.

7. George B. Reich, *The Greening of America* (New York, 1970), pp. 262-263.

3

Academies

Americans make the grievous mistake of trying to cram all formal education into a single institution, the school. They know, of course, that children learn important things from many sources—parents, peers, movies, books, schools, television, sports, churches, trips away from home, jobs, comic strips, and more. But they feel they can influence or control only one of these for the benefit of their children: the school. They leave the influence of other institutions to chance, but ask the school to fulfill its traditional academic function and as well to clean up the mess and fill the gaps resulting from the neglect of the other agencies. At some point in the future, a clever group of Americans is going to realize that the country can meet its educational ends with greater effectiveness and less waste by organizing for children a number of different settings, each appropriate for a particular purpose. Every child would have multiple "schools," as it were. Thus, we would be rediscovering the *paideia* of the Greeks, for whom the entire community was teacher, and a modern version of the colonial American educational troika of family, church, and school.

School should not be regarded essentially as a place, a building with rectangular rooms, blackboards, chalk, books, ruled paper, and teachers. Rather, it should be defined as a systematic activity of the community primarily devoted to the development of youngsters. Children can be taught in many settings; no single one is ideal for all purposes. Socrates could do with less than a garden. Outward Bound programs, devoted to developing a hearty brand of self-reliance, require wilderness, cliffs, or the sea. Retrospective studies, historical or literary, require books, artifacts, archaelogical remains. Any kind of social education calls for travel and the rubbing of shoulders with people different from oneself.

We now expect most systematic education to take place in specialized school buildings, almost all of it offered vicariously and in the abstract. Children are expected to learn how others feel by reading about them. "We studied about colored people, so now we know how they really feel." "We read about the Revolutionary War, and now we know how tyrannical George III was." "We had elections for class officers and now know how democracy works." Conventional classrooms are marvelous for some kinds of learning, but scarcely for all.

There are different *kinds* of learning, then, and each may require a particular setting. Developing an appreciation of Milton's *Paradise Lost* or the skills required for the use of chemists' balances or achieving the expressiveness of a dance or an understanding of Maoist ideology each implies a different sort of site, a staff of different sorts of adults and different expectations of how a child should behave.

There are practical limitations, obviously, to the matching up of each child with the "best" setting for him, individually, to learn a subject, or attitude, or skill, ideal though a perfect match might be. Moreover, human learning does not fall neatly into prescribed categories. A child may learn a moral lesson in a class devoted to acquiring a simple skill, or he may gain insight into logic in a setting devoted to the appreciation of the arts. Still, a different emphasis for a different situation can be useful—sufficiently so to raise serious questions about continuing all deliberate education within one formal setting.

A somewhat imperfect but useful and important line can be

drawn between education for power and education for agency and joy, as these have been defined. The first tends to be sequential, abstract, and often best undertaken privately and in a systematic manner. The second more often requires involvement in groups and participation in a wide variety of experiences. The sharpening of some powers of discrimination may demand little more than a Socratic dialogue, backed by a library. Much of science, both its substance and its internal logic, is grasped through systematic experiment in a prescribed series of problems. Communications skills are acquired through rigorous, supervised practice. Data necessary for discrimination—foreign-language skills, for example— are largely assimilated through determined, if dull and private, intellectual spadework.

Agency, on the other hand, requires the testing and involvement of a person in society. How one does in a situation is what counts. The only way a child can truly know that he can take a subway from 190th Street to Grand Central Station is to do so. Knowing that such transportation exists is largely meaningless if one cannot act on it. And action requires self-confidence, which emerges only when one has successfully coped with a new situation. One can study about the new and unfamiliar; being able to live effectively in the midst of it is far more difficult, as American soldiers from all walks of life who have been asked to live abroad know well. Too many of them came away with no feeling for those whom they arrogantly dismiss as "alien": and therein lies the kernel of American military and moral defeat, not to mention individual ignorance and misery. One cannot know the limits of one's values without testing them in some way or other.

This quality of "knowing what one can do" is especially important if one subscribes to Edward C. Banfield's persuasive categorization of class subcultures according to "distinctive psychological orientation toward providing for a more or less distant future." As he summarizes: "The more distant the future the individual can imagine and can discipline himself to make sacrifices for, the 'higher' his class."[1] The lower-class child, thus, is one who lives from minute to minute and who can see no purpose in investing in his future, by saving money or getting an education or anything else. One may presume that this condition of present-orientedness results from three causes: the expectations of his family and friends (who are behaving likewise); his lack of resources, money, and skills (which keeps him struggling to make do today); and a lack of confidence that he could, in fact, improve his lot if he did see beyond the lures of the moment. The second of these conditions is relatively easy to solve: give the youngster money and a job. The other two are more difficult, but significantly remediable through education, if steps (including immersing children in styles of life different from their own) are imaginatively and sensitively taken. Hopelessness need not be an ineradicable condition.

There is more. We are all, in different ways, bigots (which is a pejorative but useful way of saying that we all have understandable, if not always pleasing, prejudices). In what kind of check should these views be, responsibly, held? Or, at what point does the value we place on cultural pluralism supersede a deprecatory feeling we may have about some social group or other? How do these views affect other people? A person cannot really learn about himself in society without in fact being himself involved with society. The appalling rudeness of many upper-class Americans, most of whom are elegantly schooled, comes from the failure of their teachers to place them in settings where their actions provoke honest, realistic reactions. Vicarious discussion of "these other people" and elitist preaching of *noblesse oblige* are not substitutes for real, on-location testing. Children, even those from less favored homes, are given in science laboratories true

---

1. Edward C. Banfield, *The Unheavenly City: The Nature and Future of Our Urban Crisis* (Boston, 1970), pp. 46-47.

experience of the physical world, but in the social sciences they are offered only a pale, abstract imitation of reality.

As with the pedagogies associated with agency, the aspects of joy that are manifested as appreciation of beauty and as personal sensitivity require many forms of involvement, in aesthetic settings and in various groups of people. Much of joy involves a nonlogical sort of discrimination; it is intuitive, affective. It roots with difficulty, experience shows, in places where logic and system dominate. Joy in its nonrational aspect is not irrational in a senseless, anarchic way. It simply makes use of different modes of discrimination than disciplined thought alone. For these aspects of life (which traditionally have gone unrewarded), settings and conditions of a different nature from those appropriate to logical, intellectual inquiry are required. Mixing the two has usually meant that sensitivity loses out to science.

While we grant that power on one hand and agency and joy on the other overlap significantly, a practical division of institutional labor between them makes sense. Let us have *academies* primarily devoted to power. And let us have different kinds of activity—for the sake of simplicity I'll call them *collegia*—through which society may provide, deliberately and systematically, for agency and joy. *Let us have, in sum, two kinds of "schools," with children expected to attend both, often concurrently.*

Such a proposal sounds fanciful at first glance, the predictable result of excessively rational classification by a professional academic. But that is, at least in part, unfair: the record shows that this distinction between power and agency has been part of American expectations continuously for a hundred years or more. And the apparent failure of the one-school system to meet both ends could well prompt a conservative, symbol-conscious populace to act on that distinction. Two kinds of schools are not improbable in our time.

The existing school, particularly the secondary school, has

been, at heart, an academy. Charles Eliot's "main-line" subjects were designed to teach power; and the main-line subjects have survived decades of rhetorical assault. People *want* the academy. While they are less articulate about it, they also want their children to "fit in," to understand the society, and to get a "good job." They want them to have self-confidence and ambition. These ends (and the ends of personal agency, which often conflict with the will of most Americans) are, by common consent, poorly met by existing schools. The ends of power and of agency do overlap; but within our tradition the former has governed the shape of the school.

Cannot power, agency, and joy be accommodated in a single setting? Theoretically, they can, and our present system rests on this theory. Gifted teachers recognize the need for different kinds of learning and encourage them. But gifted teachers are rare; and even for them, a balance is difficult to maintain. Most teachers, even in independent boarding schools, where the rhetoric of agency is prominent, are first of all scholars—people trained to teach a subject. Only secondarily are they (if they are) skilled to foster self-confidence, autonomy, or joy. And persons adept in the latter are rarely accredited as scholars and virtually never admitted to school staffs. Academic learning is king—which is fine if one is running an academy. But if one purports to provide a comprehensive education (as most schools do), an exclusively academic staff is, on all counts, narrow and biased.

The other extreme is found in current so-called free schools and in their earlier counterparts of the Progressive era. Self-awareness, joy, and spontaneity come first there, and abstract learning occurs only secondarily, as a child explicitly expresses a desire for it. As most of the abstractions of our culture are beyond a child's experience, he has no way of knowing whether he wants them or not, and thus often gets a minimal exposure to them. The children of intellectual, mobile parents are exposed to a variety of abstractions at home, and so, not surprisingly, do far better in open settings than do those who are culturally more restricted. Some children in agency-oriented schools get as limited an education as their counterparts do in essentially power-oriented establishments.

With substantial resources and a gifted staff, it is possible to provide schools which do foster power, agency, and joy in appropriate and complementary ways. But the likelihood that any number of such schools might be available for most children is remote. It is too difficult to do; and, more important, there is an alternative way of achieving the same ends more easily. By organizing separate units for separate purposes, one removes the onus from a single teacher and school to be all things to all children. A division of labor makes it possible to accomplish all this on a large scale. And it is eminently practical.

The creation of multiple schools makes especial sense for older children, perhaps from age ten onward. Very small youngsters have enough trauma leaving home and coping with but one new setting; several would merely confuse them. A single school is clearly best for them. Such a school—usefully termed a "first school"—would self-consciously forward at once the development of power, agency, and joy, and many superb schools, such as the Sea Mills Infant School in Bristol, England, so well described by Joseph Featherstone in *Schools Where Children Learn*, succeed brilliantly.[2] However, by the time many youngsters reach age ten, they are ready for varied settings and find them often highly rewarding. Little boys especially, schooled as they are largely by women teachers, respond to activities led by imaginative men, whether "formally" in Cub Scout groups or informally "hanging around" tolerant older boys. Certainly they learn from this experience (though what they

2. Joseph Featherstone, *Schools Where Children Learn* (New York, 1971).

learn may be thoroughly antisocial). And they clearly are confident moving away from Mum's apron strings. This readiness should be seriously and sensibly provided for.

And, too, there will always be some schools for older children that might effectively teach toward the several ends within a single setting. Such is difficult to achieve, and these schools will remain the exceptions, whether they are unbelievably wealthy so-called preparatory schools or urban experiments, such as Chicago's Metro school.

Furthermore, it is worth repeating the obvious: no academy can dismiss, or undermine, learning toward agency; and no collegium can hold back or disregard a child's developing power. They will, obviously, overlap; but by emphasizing a single set of ends each—power or agency and joy—they will provide for every child the variety and quality of experience to which he has a right. If we are to sharpen our academic training and significantly improve the effectiveness of our education toward agency and joy on any kind of scale, separate institutions are necessary.

Recently, there has been much interest in "alternative schools," fresh, exciting places in which a child can learn and which can effectively compete with the public schools and, by their success, encourage reform. Even as one criticizes the strategy of their founders (similar approaches in the twenties and thirties left little mark on the majority of schools), one must particularly regret their apparent acceptance of the existing unitary school. What is needed is not an alternative model but an entirely new concept; not a competing school but a set of new, complementary settings for learning. The current school (save that for very young children) is asked to do too much, and no radical (or conservative) "alternative" within a single setting is likely to lead to a viable solution to the problem of overloading. What we need, I repeat, are not alternative schools but *complementary* schools.[3] One hopes

3. Since these paragraphs were written, there has been increased national

that the imagination and energy of present-day reformers will have more lasting and wider-scale effects than the efforts of their predecessors forty years ago; their concepts must be both (ironically) more radical and more realistic than they appear to be at the moment.

An ideal academy is one which encourages an individual to discriminate, to reason logically, and which makes available to him the skills and substantive knowledge that are the basis for the powers of discrimination and reason. It is a place of inquiry, devoted to the endless asking and answering of questions, for questioning is at the heart of discrimination. An academic child is one who knows how to analyze, to identify key issues, to question imaginatively, and to fashion relevant answers from knowledge at hand or from knowledge freshly discovered. All children have the right to be academic children, in this sense. To assert that any one child cannot learn some legitimate form of discrimination is to assign that child to slavery. He will be easily duped, imposed upon, misdirected for any manner of ends and will be prey to the designs of clever, unscrupulous leaders. In a word, he will be no better off than most of us are today. And this is as unnecessary as it is tragic. Every modern man *must* discriminate if he and we all are to survive in any kind of moral democracy. And education must see to it that every man has the opportunity to learn to do so.

Academic training does *not* mean a grasp of the approved content set down by the scholarly guilds. It is not mere mastery of subjects and it is not just aptitude for intellectual

---

political concern over the issue of court-enforced "busing" to accomplish racial or social class balance in schools. While much of this concern is misplaced, the result more of incompetent politics than of new knowledge about the negative effects of integrated schooling or of bus travel, it leads inevitably to a resurgence of "localist" feeling, of support for the neighborhood, socially and racially segregated school. In the face of this situation, the complementary, "multiple" school idea has special merit: let the kids go to their neighborhood school (academy) some of the time—and to class and race integrated schools (collegia) the rest of the time. Integrationists may today have to settle for half a loaf.

activity. It enables a person, at the very minimum, to take an abstract problem—say, a labor-management issue—and sort it out in a reasonably logical manner. He should have sufficient mathematical skill to understand, for instance, when a politician is hoodwinking him over wage claims. He should have enough sense of language and of social relations to be able to see past a man's rhetoric in public life to his true motivations. He should have some notion of how to weigh conflicting values, the claims of employers and employees, of buyers and sellers. He should have the skills to put forward clearly, if simply, his own analysis and argument orally and in writing.

One of the tragedies of the current hour is the low respect given to rigorous intellectual power. While most Americans expect schools to provide for some vague "skills of thinking," only a minority today argue that an individual's intellect serves as his best—indeed only—protection against tyranny and despair. There are several romantic and dangerous ideas abroad, often espoused, curiously, by academics who make their livings with their minds. Some imply that discriminating reason simply "happens," that a child who is educated with deliberate Rousseauan neglect will, on his own, determine the skills he needs and will, then, master them. This view confuses the chicken and the egg: if a child knows little and has no tools for learning other than random exploration, how can he possibly appreciate and act upon alternatives before him? Others argue properly that intellectual training is an imposition of teachers on children and—improperly—that any imposed teaching is ipso facto "immoral." They fail to recognize that true rationality is discriminating and critical and that a society made up of rational individuals is a society of question askers, debunkers, and problem-solvers—certainly not one of helpless drones. By "imposing" intellectual discrimination, society provides an individual with the very equipment needed to prevent all other kinds of imposition. Paradoxically, then, freedom follows from the imposed development of critical faculties.

In practice, to be sure, much of the education which is now defined as "intellectual training" may be biased and poorly suited to sharpening powers of discrimination. As has been argued earlier, power is by definition revolutionary: it leaves nothing unchallenged. And some communities do not want young, informed question-askers among them. But that some (or most) of what passes today as education of the intellect is spurious and fails to develop critical abilities does not weaken the fundamental argument: the powers of reason, of discrimination, of criticism, and of rational argument and persuasion are fundamental for citizens in a free society. Indeed, they are rights, and the society should see that they are nurtured. Neither the cold-blooded society which wants, for the benefit of an elite, to keep its citizens ill-informed and incapable of questioning nor the soft-hearted society which in an orgy of concern over the supposed "feelings" of citizens forgets they have minds is worthy.

Effective academic training for power does not mean formal education, or harshness, or ruthless imposition of adult views. Though these are the stereotypes, the opposite should be the rule. No one can learn to inquire without first becoming absorbed in a problem: academies have to be intensely interesting places, as varied as their students demand. To teach a child to analyze and distinguish takes monumental patience, and warmth and understanding. A child will hide his poor grasp of logic if he is afraid that he will be ridiculed, and if this is hidden, the teacher will have a difficult time helping the child sort things out. A reticent child can hardly be taught skills of communication; he must learn to trust and to be open with his teacher. A good academic instructor has a tricky balance to maintain: he must elicit sufficient student trust so that each pupil will be candid and open with him; at the same time, he must insist on reasonable standards of accuracy and logic. True standards rarely can be met in a hostile classroom. And standards and formality are hardly congruent. An effective class in the best academy will little resemble the tension-filled, high-status, contemporary secondary-school or college seminar.

Because individuals differ, there will always be many levels of excellence and many styles of discrimination. Some people can assimilate foreign languages easily, some not. Some "see" mathematically, some don't. Whatever the background at home, some will have more difficulty in communicating. But this cannot be used as an excuse: these are merely constraints to be adjusted to by the academies. It will not do to say that some children simply cannot learn even to some modest level of power. We cannot, morally, accept this condition, save for the obvious mental cripple.

Superficially, the curriculum of an academy would not look foreign to the best academic schoolteacher of today, though the pedagogy and respect for individual students might. The school would help a youngster to develop his ability to inquire abstractly into and to use imaginatively the principal forms of communication—languages of various kinds, including computer language, and mathematics. It would deal, too, with physical and biological scientific phenomena, and with social phenomena, past and present. And it would develop aesthetic disciplines—analytic, manual, and kinetic. These areas can be reconstrued into Eliot's "main-line" subjects, or into the classic triad of general education (sciences, social sciences, humanities), but there must be ruthless focus on process rather than coverage of official topics. Substance is necessary, and inevitable: but it must be set in a context of inquiry—of present or future *usefulness*, however abstract—lest it be simply memorized without thought and soon forgotten.

That would be the *entire* curriculum. A child could start on it virtually at birth: communication can be taught effectively at an early age, as it is now learned instinctively of course. At some point appropriate for each child (not just at five, as in the United Kingdom, or at six as in the United States, or at seven, as in some other countries), he would start attending an academy, but for no more than fifteen hours a week. He would progress as fast as his developing power allowed him, not as part of an age group. The amount of time he spent in academic work (and in concurrent involvement in collegia) would be determined, in conjunction, by himself, his parents, and his teachers. Logically, the intensity of work in both academy and collegia would vary as the youngster's changing needs and interests suggested. Systematic learning is not possible on a rigid schedule; reasonable individual flexibility is called for. (The current system allows for none at all.) The hours at academy would be intensively used. Whatever the age a child began formal academic study, he would stay (at a minimum of fifteen hours a week) until his fifteenth birthday. His progress would be tested; if he met state norms by that age, he could (if he desired) leave the academy. If he did not yet meet these norms, he would stay at it—in some form interesting to him—until he had done so.

Although tests today cannot, as critics say, test everything, they can, to a legitimate extent, test power. The principal unsolved problems facing the testing apparatus involve the qualities desired for agency. A child's progress toward power can be assessed with reasonable assurance, and his progress in the academy can be determined largely on the basis of those tests.

Academies could take many different forms. Very likely, they would use existing school buildings and much the same staff. Some communities might wish to contract out academic training to competing qualified entities; others might want a unitary system, much as we have today. Since children would be required to spend fewer hours physically in the school (but perhaps more hours actually at academic learning), there would be fewer children there at any one time. Several groups in turn would use a single facility over the course of a day. First-rate academic teaching is both difficult to plan and exhausting to carry out; teachers will need the time saved from the baby-sitting they do now to offer the kind of instruction that would be called for. With pupils progressing in significant measure on the basis of objective, or at least external, assessment, the teacher will be judged on the children's performance much more so than at present. The unsophisticated use of tests could, of course, lead to teachers trying to teach "at" these tests, and administrators might judge teacher performance in a manner as crude as that exposed by Matthew Arnold in late-nineteenth-century England. Holding instructors strictly accountable is not possible, or even very desirable. But assessing teacher effectiveness in some general manner on the basis of pupil performance, moderated by subjective review by disinterested educators over a period of time, is reasonable, at the very least to protect children from obviously incompetent teachers. An academy should avoid the extremes of guaranteed tenure (the current U.S. practice) and of narrow accountability (as with England's Revised Code of 1860). Teachers and children must both be protected.

Teaching, as B.F. Skinner has said for years, requires careful organization. Many skills are developed in a systematic and sequential pattern. Once educators identify this pattern, it can be broken up into a series of steps, each leading the student to the next. The mastery of one step provides him with the knowledge to master the following step, and so on. These patterns of steps can be programmed. The medium for a program can be a book, or a dialogue, or a computer lesson—almost anything. In many situations, a teacher actually gets in the way: the student not only can but should work alone with his program. Many good books, of course, are classic examples; there is nothing inherently mechanistic in programmed learning. It is simply a systematic approach to acquiring knowledge which can be used for many ends, even for classroom discipline, Skinner suggests. This obvious approach is still being neglected by those who run schools. Some "romantic" critics chafe at what they see as the "inhumanity" of programmed instruction. They are, of course, confusing learning for power with learning for agency and applying criteria for the one process that is relevant to the other.

Where and how a child gains power is immaterial. The time he is required to spend in an academy will not be excessive, at least by today's standards, and he will progress at his own rate—eliminating the hours wasted either waiting for his age group to catch up or listening in total confusion to the teacher expound on things he doesn't understand. He can learn from books, television, programmed materials completed on his own, playing chess, and so on: this activity will all be taken account of in the testing, as it fosters his power, his ability to discriminate. Learning builds upon learning. Some power is intuitive, of course; it entails what right-handed Jerome Bruner has happily called understanding "from the left hand." Intuitive leaps will always confound the testers and all who create developmental programs. But they can be regarded as happy exceptions, as unexpected bonuses, and, though encouraged, not counted upon. They will occur just often enough to keep our views of how power is developed modest and humble.

Teachers, largely, should control the content and pedagogy of the academy. Compared with current schools, and especially with what I call collegia, the academy has relatively few controversial spheres of study. There is more agreement among Americans regarding what power is than what, say, the content of a course on civics should be. The clash between personal and corporate values is greater in the latter than in the former. The academy considers civic issues in a relatively distant, analytic manner; collegia deal with them more directly and close-in. The difference is an important one of degree. Furthermore, the pedagogy of intellectual development can be more scientific than that applied to help a child to self-awareness and joy; thus, it is less open to interference from laymen. The academy should have at least the political insulation of the current English grammar school, and perhaps more. It should be the creature of state government, rather than of the particular community it serves.

Power is achieved in many places, even the commercial entertainment industry. The communications media entertain and inform. That they teach is a truism. That they distort and cheapen our culture is a cliché. The surprise is that few Americans have ever regarded them as school.

Television is the key communications medium. There are TV sets in virtually every American home, and they are on for several hours a day on the average. Programs for children were seen as staple fare from the very beginning of commercial broadcasting, but until recently the shows have been either mawkish and excessively commercialized or starved for resources, or both. The huckstering of Bozo, the Clown is repellent; much of what Robert Keeshan does as Captain Kangaroo is very worthwhile; and the warmth of Mister Rogers comes through because of his low-key, simple approach. Few programs until *Sesame Street*, however, seriously considered specific educational ends and developed a careful pedagogy, appropriate to the medium, to achieve them. Although the evidence is only now coming in, the effectiveness of *Sesame Street* is so evident that it already stands as a firm example of what can be done for children over television.

Much of *Sesame Street* is aimed at power, and not surprisingly so. Television provides only vicarious experience, and agency requires extensive real experience. However, the interracial cast, the careful selection of a city setting, and the use by the actors of various dialects bring the program within the experience of the less advantaged city children, and it is with them that the program has had most significant effect.

Why not more *Sesame Streets*, for all ages? In fact, most of the current experiments are in adult education; none seri-

ously serve adolescents. The British have just launched the
Open University, a full-scale, degree-granting enterprise with
its own vice-chancellor and full-time staff. It aims at adults
who missed, for any of a variety of reasons, the chance to
enter higher education immediately after secondary school,
and it is appropriately termed the university of "the second
chance." Every one of the 25,000 places for candidacy in the
first year was instantly snapped up. The courses, leading
toward a B.A., are conducted over television and radio;
reading and written assignments are completed at home; and
tutorials are held in centers scattered over the United Kingdom. Though the Open University is not geared to, nor does
it purport to teach, the gentlemanly ideal, as the residential
colleges in traditional English universities have done, it can
teach toward intellectual power. By *Sesame Street* standards,
the program-courses are dull, little more than filmed lectures
which make poor use of the medium; but the potential is
there. If Open University objectives could be combined with
the production techniques of Rowan and Martin's *Laugh-In*
(one of the few television programs that fully utilize the
medium), a step would have been taken in adult programming comparable to the advance made by *Sesame Street* over
Romper Room. Lord Clark's remarkable series, *Civilisation*,
shows what might be done (though *Civilisation*'s sophistication guarantees it a limited audience). There have been
experiments in the United States in this area, of course, such
as the undergraduate program filmed for the Navy by the
Boston Area Commission on Extension Studies, the plans for
an open university experiment in New York state, and the
high-quality, one-shot exercises of *CBS Reports.* But the
efforts have been limited, seriously underfunded, and not
given the kind of backing that the British Open University
has enjoyed.

Of course, television is already teaching. Given its dependence on advertising, it must please enough of the people
enough of the time to keep the corporate sponsors of

programming happy. Television must entertain; most Americans must like (or be made to like) most of the shows. These shows, then, must reinforce the values of most Americans; they must cater to the American ego. But discrimination results from egos that have been "shaken" rather than catered to. The mass media provoke fresh thinking when they jar, when they present the unfamiliar or show a familiar object from a new angle. One reflects on the beneficial influence that Wiesman's brutally honest film *High School*, if widely seen, might have on the views of most Americans regarding secondary education. CBS's *Hunger in America* clearly had an effect, jolting viewers into seeing a situation which was before their very eyes but which they had completely missed. One learns a process of judgment by having to judge among alternatives. But the media today give us few. If television is to teach in the fullest sense, it must have variety, not only a variety of political viewpoints (which so exercises Spiro Agnew) but variety on more homely issues, such as advertising. Ralph Nader and the Consumers' Union should get something like equal time with merchants, just as the American Cancer Society and the Surgeon General were given equal time with a little pressure from the federal government to rebut cigarette advertising. Minority groups need to have their say, as much to teach the majority (albeit through discomfort) as to entertain and instruct their own people. Television, which can teach only vicariously, can provide data, images, sensation, information. The more varied these are, the greater is the likelihood that they will help people assimilate many values and lead people to use their good sense in making judgments. If it is clearly in the public interest that variety be offered, and if the private sector cannot finance it, then public resources must be utilized for the purpose.

In view of the immense power of television, it is surprising that Americans have left it almost entirely in the hands of the profit makers. There is nothing wrong with commercial enterprise in communications as such; but some socially desirable activities can never make a monetary profit. Their payoff is far subtler, as in the case of schools themselves. (Though some critics today feel that even schools would improve if they had to make a profit, the trustees of American private schools and universities and the directors of corporations in what is called the "ed biz" know it isn't all that simple.) If television can achieve certain educational goals at a markedly lower cost than can other institutions, such as nursery schools, the public should insist on appropriate screening time, either over public television or over commercial channels. If effectiveness increases with a combination of television, books, and other learning materials, then a package, produced and distributed at public expense, would be desirable. Indeed, "packages" not at all tied to television might be made available: some of the subsidized printed materials in the British Open University, for example, can stand on their own. Such programs might still be less costly than formal schools and have far more impact.

An educational system which allowed an individual to progress on the basis of his demonstrated intellectual performance (rather than on time served in school houses) would encourage the serious use of what are now called "informal" agencies of education. In fact, of course, sensitive television and publishing are *schools*; more specifically, they are legitimate forms of academies. While they can rarely stand on their own, as almost every learner needs the give and take of a tutor and sensible counsel of those more experienced than he, they can complement, in a remarkably efficient way, "formal" study. For Americans to continue to ignore this potential is an extraordinary waste.

A free culture in an advanced technology requires informed, discriminating citizens. The academy should be devoted exclusively to this purpose (while, of course, not

undermining those of agency and joy). It should be comple-
mented by opportunities for students through the various
informal media. The society should guarantee to each citizen
(other than the obvious mental cripple) the right to powers
of discrimination and should provide responsible tests to
assure this individual and his family that such are achieved in
as flexible, efficient, and imaginative a way as possible.

4

Collegia

Few parents fail to hope that their children will become self-confident, dependable, happy, and useful people—to wit, to have a sense of "agency" and control over their lives. What is remarkable is how ineptly we act upon these hopes, how little serious energy we give to the deliberate education we devote to them. Providing for a new kind of school heavily biased toward agency is a likely way to begin. Thus, a *collegium.*

Why that term? Because it is presumptuous, and presumptuous words attract attention, and sometimes even status. Because much of agency is learned in groups, and a "college" in its original and enduring meaning is a group. It has been used in Anglo-American formal education for over eight centuries. The colleges of the ancient English universities, their American counterparts, and various elite schools, most of them boarding schools which have flourished in the English-speaking world, gave great weight, perhaps even excessive weight, to the "pastoral care" of their young charges. "Character" was key. The English Grammar School and university college was devoted in large part to fashioning gentlemen, men of manners and taste. It was, in today's jargon, an elaborate commune and attempted to instill a set of values, a task which the reader of history must grant it accomplished remarkably well.

For our day, however, there can be no one college model, no single, ideal collegium, for diversity here is paramount. The collegium must address the legitimate contradictions inherent in any education for agency, the conflicting claims of the individual and the state. The individual properly desires autonomy and personal freedom. The state properly wants a stable population, one disposed to advance corporate social and economic ends. It is unlikely that the aims of each can be fully met within a single institution. Both have to be taught (if one truly believes in individual and social rights), but the resolution of conflicting claims must be left to the individual alone .Resolutions cannot be imposed, either by an agent of the individual (a counselor selected by him) or by the state (the teacher, the employee of the school board who, despite all talk of academic freedom, is readily affected by that board's expectations). The society can, and properly should, teach powers of discrimination—the task of the academy—but it should leave the implementation of this power to the individual.

Children can be helped to acquire self-awareness and a personal set of values. Through a series of experiences—some vicarious, some simulated, some real—a child can see at first hand how society works (or appears to work) and how he reacts to it. Currently, he is *told* how the system operates, he is told at least what its presumed values are, and he is told how he is to fit in. If he were allowed to learn in a real situation—by accompanying a police officer for a week, for example—he could sense in his own way the difficulties and strains of that role. If, in addition to first-hand experience with the police, sensitive discussion were provided, led by adults who are both knowledgeable about security work and aware of the concerns of children, the chances are high that society will make its case *and* the student will assimilate the reality of the situation (not just what a teacher *says* its reality is). A youngster who has had a series of such experiences, each guided by different adults with different kinds of commitments, would be less susceptible to narrow, imposed values. Put another way, the student would learn from a series of schools, each offering certain values and knowledge but without a consistent, overall ideology, except to have the child understand. The state could hardly be expected to sponsor collegia involving violent revolution, however: the extremes of experience would, realistically, be excluded.

Some of these operations would be of short duration, such as a fortnight accompanying a policeman. Others might last longer, such as membership in an orchestra. Some might involve travel; others might involve participation in a discussion group. Some authority, perhaps attached to the academy—or, better still, an independent enterprise—would coordinate the collegia and act as adviser to parents and children. Every child between five and sixteen years of age would take part in one or another activity, or in several, for at least forty hours a month. An individual counselor would assist him, and his parents, to select among them a range of possibilities and would hold a continuing discussion with the youngster.

Some will scoff: is *this* education? All children get this kind of experience anyway: that is what we say. But of course *they do not.* Even the most favored children sometimes live sheltered, narrow lives and are fearful of the unknown and of change and never acquire self-confidence. One need only watch the rich and the poor endure basic military training to see how narrow and fragile most boys' youthful experience is. And one can guess that girls' experiences might be even more restricted. A child has a right to wide experience; and society has an obligation to provide it in a calculated, sensitive manner. Teachers (or whatever those who labor in a collegium might be called) should assist children, supporting and counseling them as they learn to cope with the new and frightening and as they build a sense of their own competence and confidence. This kind of help should not be left to chance; it can be systematically provided for. As such, it is education.

At the same time, others will protest that yet another "school" is an affront to children's freedom. It is an "imposed" institution, they will argue, and will quickly inherit all the conservative, dehumanizing, and bureaucratic ills of the existing public school system. What we should rather do, as Ivan Illich puts it, is to "disestablish school" and to replace it with a loose system of what he calls "learning webs," over which the individual youngster has some control (though the webs, of course, are "imposed" by his elders).[1] However, the collegium need not be bureaucratic, in the pejorative sense, and it can be kept dynamic; it can, in its many versions, teach a variety of values; and it can, if imaginatively organized, draw on many kinds of people as teachers, not just those who are technically "certified." In sum, it can meet some of Illich's objections to formal education. However, what it does *not* do is to leave certain opportunities for learning to chance, which is what total "deschooling" would do. It makes options available and insists that at least some are tried. It "imposes" society's wish that no child be wholly cloistered, cut off, ghettoed. Leaving all of education beyond simple skill training to chance is a recipe for narrow bigotry. Or so our recent history can be read.

Examples of systematic activity that can advance differing aspects of a child's sense of agency are almost limitless. The truism that youngsters learn to tolerate and understand people different from themselves by meeting and working with such people has now been substantiated by the social sciences, which have found that children from poor homes assimilate middle-class ways if they are schooled with middle-class children. In view of this, programs to bring together youngsters of different races and social classes seem especially important, particularly in areas where total school integration by class and race is, practically or politically, unfeasible. Children could go to their neighborhood academy, which for logistic reasons might have to be relatively

1. Ivan Illich, *Deschooling Society* (New York, 1970).

segregated. But then, twice a week and every third weekend, they would take part in a common project—caring for the aged, park cleanups, and so forth—in deliberately integrated groups. The primary emphasis would be on completing the project, but the pedagogical aim would be to teach children to get along with one another, even with children quite different from themselves. Integration, in the sense of decreased prejudice and greater awareness and tolerance of groups different from our own, remains an essential aim of American society. It is primarily a matter of agency, and it can best be learned by experience—ergo, a collegium expressly designed to that end.

Another kind of enterprise that could provide a sense of agency is the child-care center. Such centers are in obvious demand, and older children particularly benefit from work with infants. They gain perspective on their own growth and development; they can also pick up practical information that would be of use to them as prospective parents; and, under supervision, they can be of real help even at a young age. That is, they can be "needed"; a ten-year-old boy can "help" a two-year-old at a very meaningful level. And it is good for both of them, as anyone who has watched children can testify. Since many older people with extensive first-hand experience with youngsters desire part-time employment, one can envision day-care centers that mix generations—infants to grandparents—and thus teach them all.

Several striking examples of nascent collegia come from Australia.[2] The emphasis on pastoral care at the Geelong Grammar School under the great Sir James Darling is legendary. Darling had his boys mount a substantial school building project each year, in the belief that the process of physical construction was a fine means to teach respect for honest labor and the limits of human effort. The Geelong site has gates, and walls, and buildings put up by boys. Most impres-

2. The Australian examples are drawn from my experience teaching in Victoria in 1958.

sive is the school's Timbertop annex, in the mountains in the east of Victoria. Darling arranged for every intermediate level (in American terms, tenth grade) boy to spend the entire year at this wilderness site with his teachers. The boys built virtually all the small houses in which they live, in small groups. Athletics consists (or did so in the days of Darling) of bushcraft and of endurance trials of gradually increasing severity culminating in a mandatory, twenty-six mile marathon run. The boys are left on their own much of the time; they are to learn from experience in nature how to cope with themselves and with their colleagues.

Boys were admitted to Geelong not so much on the basis of intellectual capacity as on their parents' ability to pay the high fees. Accordingly, the student body in the fifties was intellectually diverse but socially homogenous. This didn't bother Darling; as he put it, "rich boys have souls too." His job was to deepen and toughen boyish liveliness into manly virtue. The school chaplain played a predictable part in Darling's plan; more unusual was the work of an assistant master, John Bechervaise.

In the late fifties, Bechervaise—a scientist, humanist, and explorer of Antarctica and Australia's center—was given complete charge of a group of academically inept sixth-formers, boys who in Australia would probably not be in school at all. They were the sons of rich country families and had been left with Darling for "finishing." Bechervaise put each on his own, tried to find each boy's special interest and then build on that. He had boys painting and surveying and writing. A boy might start with a farming problem. Bechervaise would carry this into agronomy and the related sciences. He would have the boy write about his work, sketch it, prepare maps, plot related weather projections, and so on. Bechervaise's own remarkably broad education was pushed to the limit, of course. He had to know a great deal about a great many fields. He ran what educators call a "problem-centered" program, but it had at its core not so much a concern for a boy to cover an academic subject as for that boy to gain self-confidence and self-esteem in completing a piece of meaningful research. While he had inevitably a concern for power, he was primarily interested in agency, and on behalf of boys who had been badly scarred by repeated failure in highly academic grammar schools. Judging by the élan and interest of the boys, Bechervaise did succeed in building self-esteem. Whether the boys could spell or cipher was of secondary importance.

Sir Brian Hone, Darling's counterpart in the Melbourne Grammar School, made the dual concern for power and agency quite explicit, as is the case in many English Public Schools. All teachers were expected to be both scholars and model gentlemen, but they were promoted for special excellence in either. One route up led to the post of Department Chairman; the other, that of House Master. To oversimplify: the first had prime responsibility for the intellect; the second for the soul. Hone, a giant of a man in every respect, presided over Australia's preeminent academic school—his scholars won prizes by the bushel—but he endlessly stressed what he and others have called pastoral care. Conduct was the key: Hone would readily forfeit a football match for his school if just one boy even modestly questioned an umpire's call.

Hone's and Darling's schools had problems, obviously. Their concept of good conduct was elitist and inflexible. To the extent that it was shaped by the Church of England, it was doctrinaire. The practice of having older boys supervise younger ones sometimes led to psychic, if not physical, cruelty. There was too much intolerance—the insensitive snobbery of the elect. Furthermore, at least at Melbourne Grammar, the intellect came first. Hone's able academic staff put science before souls, and in spite of chapel services, the House system, prefects, a Cadet Corps, Boy Scouts, and all the familiar paraphernalia for "character training," most boys made it, or didn't, solely on the basis of examination results. Melbourne and Geelong represent two different ways to address agency and power, and they exemplify how unwise it is to try to provide for them both within a single institution, where one must then be favored at the expense of the other.

A highly influential modern innovator is the German refugee schoolmaster, Kurt Hahn.[3] Building self-confidence, self-awareness, and a sense of one's own strength and limitations is at the core of Hahn's philosophy. Boys and girls must meet physical challenges and learn to overcome them. Physical challenge here is a metaphor for spiritual challenge: if one learns to "make it" down a cliff, if one sees how far one can truly extend oneself, if one learns how to depend on others within a team in a test of physical courage and stamina, then one will call upon these resources in dealing with emotional and intellectual problems. If the physical trials are related to a social need—manning a lifeboat along a dangerous coast, for example—so much the better. The lesson of selflessness will be that much more marked.

The Outward Bound schools, one of the institutional extensions of Hahn's ideas, provide programs exclusively devoted to character building. The organization does not have schools in the sense of academies; it has pure collegia. It offers courses for boys, and sometimes girls, at sites providing physical tests—in mountains, in Wales or in the American Rockies; in wild lake country, as in northern Minnesota; at sea, off the coast of Maine or, until recently, at Fourah Bay in Cameroon. At each site, a youngster must learn to work with a team (rowing together in a lifeboat, for example); to deal with fear (the chronicle of the terror of the desert-dwelling northern Nigerian boys being marched into the sea at Cameroon is poignant); and to learn to cope for oneself (at the end of most programs, each youngster is outfitted with a few tools and some food and lives alone in the wilderness for several days).

One can extend beyond Hahn's creations, of course, and

3. Robert Skidelsky, *English Progressive Schools* (Hammondsworth [U.K.], 1969), part 4.

visualize other kinds of challenges, or brushes with "new conditions." Self-confidence can only emerge from experience with the unfamiliar, and such need not only be those found in nature. Some perhaps more prosaic examples—but often no less challenging and even initially terrifying—might involve a country child living for a spell with a family in a city, and vice versa. Or an American child might live in Mexico, and vice versa (a kind of collegium long conducted by the Experiment in International Living). A group of children might debate controversial social and political issues with various groups, some chosen for their deliberate hostility. (Such an enterprise could be argued as part of an academy as well). Youngsters might carry out specific tasks in unfamiliar settings alone or in small groups: making purchases in stores in another part of a city, visiting sick and elderly people regularly over a large area, serving as messengers for a dispersed business.

Middle America has a plethora of schools for agency, or at least facsimiles thereof. We have Boy Scouts, Girl Scouts, Cubs, and Brownies; in a different context, the 4-H Clubs; all kinds of youth and social-service groups, many associated with churches; and many more. Pedagogically (if one can usefully use that word in this context), many of these organizations are simplistic and ideological. There are oaths, and promises, and vows, all to be memorized the way one memorizes at school (meaning the academy). The approach hardly matches Hahn's for sophistication, and the effort may be limited, but the mass appeal of these institutions underscores both their importance to children and the political and financial support they enjoy among adults. Helping kids is a good thing. And helping them, in these contexts, means assisting them to fit in as useful members of society.

One enterprise of vast size, even though it almost exclusively serves the middle class, is the camping movement. Its rhetoric is full of the clichés of agency: character building, man-making, the building of confidence, and all the rest. A great deal of what camps attempt is effective, particularly in that a child is removed for a brief period from his home environment. It is often his first experience in unfamiliar surroundings, and this is frightening and challenging. Properly handled, it can be highly educational. But camping often depends excessively on the judgment of very young counselors, persons who themselves are only just finding out who they are and are scarcely sensitive to the fright of a small child that's just left Mama. Moreover, camps are prone to the rah-rah team spirit that, when excessive, corrupts organized sport.

Camps can easily correct the first situation and improve on the second if they have more resources that would permit them to employ an experienced staff in the necessary numbers. Camps can be permanent sites for collegia; there is no reason why so many lie idle eight months of the year or more. A camp is a school for agency and should operate full-time. It surely can serve other functions than merely to allow upper-middle-class parents to get rid of the kids for the summer.

Other kinds of enterprises have sharper, or more limited, focuses. An example is the Junior Achievement programs, which help high-school youngsters to establish and manage small, transitory businesses. A youngster learns how to be an entrepreneur by being one, assisted and supervised by an experienced businessman. He learns practical economics, but more important to many supporters of the programs, he develops self-confidence and a sense of his own abilities. The structure and aims of Junior Achievement and those of the "producing" schools envisioned by James Coleman mentioned previously—schools that are primarily producers of economic and social goods and services and only secondarily vehicles for the assimilation of learning by children—are in interesting respects very much alike.

Many social-service enterprises, some now operated by schools, provide help to people in trouble and at the same time develop a sense of worth for a child. The Wanstead County High School in London, for example, designs and fabricates special equipment for physically handicapped children and old people. Other schools, both elementary and secondary, run various kinds of programs for invalids or "shut-ins," to great effect. The youngster who, after several months of reading to an elderly blind person, realizes that he needs that person as much as the person needs him has learned something valuable both about himself and about others. Many of these enterprises are poorly managed and haphazard, but some are clearly nascent collegia of considerable worth.

Influenced particularly by radical-romantic educational critics, a new kind of secondary school, one "without walls," is growing in popularity. A prominent example is Philadelphia's well-publicized Parkway School, a high school that uses for its sites the museums, offices, and laboratories of the city's center. Students become a part of the life of those real institutions and learn first-hand of the life and work within them. Although Parkway purports to foster both power and agency, agency appears to many to predominate. The city-as-school concept supports well the intuitive and interactive kind of learning that leads to agency. It is probably not as successful at providing the sequential, often private activity which is characteristic of the best of academy. Parkway and its offshoots in other communities show how youngsters can come to self-awareness in a wide variety of adult settings; they prove that it is possible to let children test their interests and abilities in the adult world without fear. (The child who makes a wrong judgment about his first job is fired; in a Parkway-type school a first immersion in a real work-a-day setting allows for failure.)

There are more radical versions of Parkway, such as Trout Fishing in America, in Cambridge, Massachusetts. This enterprise encourages school dropouts to join its various groups and to learn in company with a number of cooperative craftsmen-teachers in the city. A participant sets out to learn both a craft and the love of craftsmanship. And as with John Bechervaise's sixth-formers, it is hoped that the student will be aroused by an interest in the particular craft to explore beyond it. By joining an adult at work at his craft, the youngster can see a clear connection between skill (manual, artistic, and intellectual) and a tangible, worthwhile result. There is then no gulf in his mind between the vicarious learning of school and the real world. They are one and the same. In addition, all those who are part of Trout Fishing, both the adults and the youths, act as a sort of family which can help, stimulate, and love the individual. Enterprises such as Trout Fishing are largely new, and their long-term effectiveness cannot yet be gauged. Their finances and their leadership are precarious and lead to frequent collapses; few of these groups have had the staying power to survive for long. (Their transience may not necessarily be a bad thing, however, since the spirit of these efforts comes from their very newness. It is difficult to picture Trout Fishing as a bureaucratic, tradition-encrusted entity.) These "schools" do attract and seem to work for individuals with whom no Boy Scout troop, much less a conventional educational institution, could come to terms.

The federal government, concerned over the talent lost to society because of poverty, organized in the mid-sixties what it calls Upward Bound programs to identify able low-income teenagers of high academic potential but average performance and help them to succeed. Upward Bound is a perfect example of the clash, in practice, of the ends of power and agency. The rhetoric of the program encompasses both, and joy, too, but when all is said and done, the criteria for success is the admission of Upward Bound graduates to college. The programs try to help the "whole" child but are judged on their success in producing an "academic" child. If the continuation of an Upward Bound program depends on success so defined, it behooves its director to admit only kids

who will, almost surely, get into college. High-risk participants endanger future funding. Helping a child to pull himself
together is not enough, it appears, unless pulling himself
together includes continued further academic or vocational
study. Not even a respectable job counts. It would be better
for Upward Bound to strive for both power and agency, not
one or the other, but in any case it needs to emphasize
agency, as the existing schools will go on emphasizing
academic power. (If they do not do so effectively, however,
the answer is not an appended special program such as
Upward Bound, but a reformed school *in toto*.) The worst of
the present situation, however, is that the contradictions
between the aims stated and the criteria for success are
glossed over. Everyone pretends they do not exist.

While much of a person's powers of adaptability is only
learned through direct experience, sometimes vicarious exercises using simulations of real experience are useful (and, too,
they often serve the ends of power simultaneously). One kind
of experience, useful in the academy as in the collegium,
involves a series of planning exercises, organized as a game.
Certain facts of a situation are provided—say, data on a town
and a number of future projections of its population growth
and composition—and varying futures explored. The effects
of each future can be built into the game, so that the players
can see graphically and experience vicariously the implications of their actions. Simulation games are now used in
the training schools of the armed services and in business;
Buckminster Fuller has devised an elaborate *World Game*
which purports to teach adaptability and control of change.

Seeing an issue through eyes different from one's own can
teach complexity. This kind of learning can be done vicariously, often through literature. Arthur Miller's salesman
brings us close to one kind of experience, King Lear does to
another. But literary abstractions do not move some children;
only actual participation can. Work in a hospital, with the
patients and with the staff, opens up new perspectives. Being

systematically exposed over several weeks to the action in a municipal court or in the mayor's office or to life in a family on welfare can "teach." The schoolgirls who exposed the horrors of nursing homes for Ralph Nader learned, not only from their investigations, but from performing a clearly needed public service. The collegium student can be a useful producer as well as consumer.

The arts contribute to one's sense of agency, for they are forms of communication which can be extraordinarily enriching. One learns about oneself as one attempts to express oneself. And when self-expression is sensitively criticized and encouraged, it leads to understanding. The academy would provide art skills and discipline, but the collegium would go far beyond. Painting, design, filmmaking, photography, the dance, drama, woodwork, leatherwork, and so on, are all vehicles for self-awareness, but not if they are overly formal (paint as I, the teacher, paints; admire what I admire), or mawkish and trivial (gee whiz, children, just go on and *express* yourselves!). The arts today have nowhere near the sustained support they need. They exist extracurricularly and are available largely to the well-to-do. They are regarded as frills, not as a serious means to help children understand themselves and communicate in significant ways. Sissy stuff. It will be difficult indeed to smash these stereotypes.

For some children, group therapy, or even individual help, can be highly rewarding educationally. Where experience in social service or in the arts provides an indirect, and subtle, awakening of personality, direct work on "who one is" can be very useful. Many wealthy youngsters are given professional counseling; others would probably benefit from it, too. While some of the therapy is aimed at remedying a harmful condition, it can also be liberating, contributing to one's sense of agency.

Finally, there is athletics. At their best, competitive sports are a useful means of "testing"—a corporate Outward Bound. Noncompetitive sports—hiking, for example—can also open the child's eyes to new possibilities. Both the process of learning, say, how to skate, and the process of enjoying the use of that skill in hockey are enriching. While we rightly mock the Dink Stover athlete-hero, and while sports-for-the-crowd's-sake fully deserve the criticism heaped on them, the value of athletics aimed exclusively at the benefit of young participants is surprisingly underrated. Academic snobs short-sightedly joke about the "jocks" and take a nap when the primeval need for exercise is felt. Neither this attitude nor the overprotective rah-rah tradition of much of school and Little League sports should blind us to the possibilities of wise athletic programs for children.

Examples of operations for agency abound; we need cite no more. They are being tried virtually everywhere, in some way; but most have serious flaws. Too many are associated with a particular social class or group, or have taken on stultifying symbolism. Tennis is for the rich; work with young children, for girls. Professors' sons aren't Boy Scouts; that's for the sons of car dealers. Art is for girls and, as they cruelly say, for fairies. If a boy has to be musical, the trumpet, clarinet, or tuba will do—with the electric guitar for the less square. Violins are for girls. Self-conscious talk about oneself is a sign of weakness, of being kooky or a gossip. Lending a hand to policemen or firemen is for the lower-middle-class children of policemen and firemen. Children from higher-income families may work in hospitals, even in the most menial jobs, because they may one day be big-shot doctors. Educationally effective though these activities can be, they can lose most of their impact if thus stereotyped.

Not everyone responsible for these kinds of enterprises gives serious thought to a pedagogy to meet the needs of different children; not everyone is as careful and systematic as those who operate Outward Bound. Many programs suffer from elegant posturing: the badge craze of the Scouts; the *noblesse oblige* snobbery of some social-service enterprises; the plumed puffery of school bands; the narcissistic braggadocio of the school sports teams; the saccharine, undiscriminating quality of art shows. Many of these antics have a good side. Uniforms give a kind of pride; the growls of school athletes are expressions (however ludicrous) of growing self-confidence. Often, however, the original purpose is lost; the end becomes empty winning, or cruelty to prove one's manhood, or forced rehearsing to impress an audience. Sometimes, too, the pedagogy is self-conscious, even wrong-headed and harmful. The well-intentioned but misled T-group can be a waste of time, or worse.

The simple fact is that not enough educators have seriously explored how agency can be developed. Much of the work springs from hunches, from direct experience, but without serious evaluation, even of a subjective sort. As long as this kind of activity is treated as an add-on, it will not attract the attention of a substantial number of educators and scholars. If the collegium is to be considered seriously, sophisticated pedagogies of some weight are needed.

Virtually all these activities are financially starved and operate with little continuity, with the notable exception of some sports activities and some work supported by the public schools. Art and music schools are in a chronic state of crisis. And given their cost, most activities are simply not available to the children of the poor. With the exception, again, of some spectator sports, the very enterprises that might best serve children in developing a sense of agency are not open to them. Ironically, when the existing system continues to fail to do this kind of teaching, the reaction of the public is simply to curse it. No one seems to have noticed that schools, their laudable academic aims notwithstanding, are poorly structured to foster agency on a comprehensive basis, and that other institutions, many already in existence, can do it better. School is school; if it doesn't happen in that school building, it isn't education. The waste is unnecessary.

In sum, the development of agency requires varied experience, not just that available in one geographical place. It requires the guidance and friendship of many kinds of adults and colleagues, not just those adults interested and skilled in academic teaching. It does not lend itself often to sequential learning and formal testing, as it is as likely as not to be intuitive and is judged better in real action than with words about action. A grasp of agency may develop over certain stages, but it is not directly related to age; exclusive contact with those of similar age is both illogical and harmful. Some self-possessed people (that is, ones with agency) are inept academicians, and vice versa. The forced alliance of education for power and for agency may retard one at the expense of the other. While one cannot run a school exclusively for power (for the acquisition of power often leads to agency, and how any school treats its students affects their view of themselves), nor exclusively for agency (it is impossible to isolate anything totally from intellectual discrimination), separate enterprises with more focused and creative emphases make obvious good sense.

To repeat: power and agency cannot be wholly separated. A child learns about himself as he develops powers of discrimination, and he sharpens his intellect as he grapples with issues of society and his place within it. However, systematic efforts to assist a child to learn each do not follow similar patterns. Power most often requires sustained, sequential, and quite private effort. Agency requires corporate experience and development which is as much intrinsic as deliberate. Sites and the kind of staff needed for one differ, obviously, from what would best serve the other. Save for very young children, two overlapping but distinct "schools" are needed.

We must abolish the existing school and create two to replace it: an academy for power, and a collegium for agency. A specific staff would be hired for each, and a program designed for each purpose. And the state would support and honor both.

If the creation of dual, or multiple, schools were politically unlikely, the same ends might be met in a less threatening and pretentious way. Shorten the current school day to three hours. Concentrate, in school, intensively and exclusively on ends for power. The shortened day would give teachers more time to prepare for teaching, and there would be smaller classes, the children attending in shifts. In addition, make available to the children half-day options in accredited "associated activities," coordinated by the school, to an extent housed at the school, and centered on existing programs among social-service groups, with museums and similar organizations.

Either way, the child would have at least two schools and probably more—several places in which to succeed or fail. His development would not depend entirely on one school or, as for far too many elementary-school children, on one class-room alone. There would be variety, and places that honor and respect different values, skills, and behavior. Though the goals of power and agency overlap, the differences would be emphasized. Different educational approaches, differing ped-agogies, would come into play, and the child would benefit from this diversity not only in the variety thus offered to him, but in the broader experiences made possible.

Employability is, of course, a central part of agency. The society needs a balanced and skilled labor force; an individual needs a source of income which is not only sufficient to support him and his dependents but which is also intrinsically rewarding. For most employment, one needs power: to that extent, the academy is a vocational school. Most jobs require self-awareness, confidence, and adaptability: to that extent collegia are vocational. Few youngsters get a true "feel" for likely avenues of employment, however, without direct ex-perience. As the skills required in many industries change rapidly, much relevant training can be had only on the job. Few schools can maintain the modern equipment and trained staff required to prepare for a wide range of jobs, whether blue-collar or white-collar.

Quite obviously, then, vocationally oriented education

should be carried out on location. This would include training in technical skills, as in vocational education as we have it today, but it would go further. Youngsters should have the opportunity to sample various career options. In some situations, they should be able to work regularly for pay, not only to learn a particular trade but to gain generally useful experience in being employed, taking responsibility, and being part of a corporate system. They would be engaged in the learning of doing. The line between classic, on-the-job vocational training and collegia is vague. Business (and government) should provide the former without charge and should be persuaded to provide the latter at public expense. Jobs would be broadly defined, of course. On-the-job training for baby-sitting (that is, child care) would revolve around a "business" consisting of a group of families, the "job supervisor" being a public-health nurse supported part-time for this purpose with state funds. The point is that not all jobs suitable for this kind of training are industrial. Fresh thought and imaginative pedagogies are needed to improve education that opens up avenues to different occupations. Our present vocational training is too tightly bound to current skills and focuses insufficiently on adaptability. And scant attention is given to the psychological and moral aspects of working.

An "occupation" that brought grief to many Americans in the 1960's was military service resulting from the draft. Some men were called, some were not. The system of selection was full of inequities, discriminating against young men with low incomes as blatantly as do the schools. Several important factors are involved in any consideration of military conscription, and all have a bearing in one way or another on education. One is the justice of the method used to select some for service instead of others. Another is the extent of a youth's right not to fight in a war on grounds of conscience. A third is the wisdom of a volunteer army, the alternative to conscription. And a fourth, most important, is the extent of a citizen's obligation to provide himself (his time, not just his money through taxes) for public service.

The first three are largely beyond the scope of this book. Let us review them briefly, however. A reasonable national policy of conscription would be one of complete equity: everyone who is able to serve somehow and somewhere should do so. Persons with skills in nationally critical trades would serve in those trades: doctors as doctors, experts on China in intelligence and public affairs; and so forth. On the second point, no youth should be required to kill or help to kill if he finds that act abhorrent on moral grounds. He can serve in another capacity, if not as a rifleman, at least as an orderly, say, in a mental hospital. An all-volunteer army—the third point—would be as dangerous as it probably is impractical. War is the politics of last resort; those who see its practice as essential for their personal esteem have been the plague of history. While it is true that the American professional army in the 1930's remained strictly the servant of civil government, the growth of military influence since World War II suggests that that posture may require more forebearance on the part of the military than in earlier times. The army needs skilled men who are, nonetheless, hostile to the use of military force save as a last resort. Many professional soldiers are of this mind, of course; but the international record of power ill-used by generals and their loyal standing armies is chilling. America can do without a version of the Greek colonels, or any other such self-appointed saviors. We must have first-rate armed forces staffed with discriminating, thoughtful men, a substantial number of them noncareerists. There must always be a goodly corps of men who can afford to say no.

The fourth point has special significance when seen in the light of the first three. Many services of unquestionable public importance require substantial manpower. The army is one such service, but only one. American hospitals have a desperate need for orderlies. Hundreds of thousands of elderly and infirm people could live comfortably and quite independently if they had the regular, if limited, help of some modestly trained responsible adults. The environment could be improved immeasurably by an organized effort to clean up after our more uncouth countrymen, or to protect and maintain what limited wilderness we have left, much as the Civilian Conservation Corps was designed to do in the 1930's. Infants and young children require and deserve extravagant attention: effective collegia, particularly for small children, for instance, call for many adults with many skills, sometimes just the "skill" of feeling concern and affection for children. The need for people to "go into service" is almost infinite. We need an army, and, sensibly, we conscript for it. With equal force, we need hospital orderlies, teachers, and more. Why not conscript for them too?

Two important aspects of education for agency are supervised experience in unfamiliar settings and the chance to produce a needed good or service. Learning to adapt to a new situation comes from doing just that, but the jolt can be made less harsh by careful planning and counseling. The joy of being needed is almost universal: witness the enthusiasm of the early Peace Corps volunteers, who found (they thought) something useful and humane that they could *do*. For many men, military service provides a remarkable educating experience, distasteful though the need for an armed force might be to many of them. The travel involved in the Peace Corps and the military (particularly when it does not involve actual fighting, as it does not for the overwhelming majority of American servicemen) is, like it or not, broadening. VISTA puts young people in surroundings markedly different from those they have known in the past. It is, in a way, an Outward Bound kind of experience, primarily for the benefit of someone else.

The obvious conclusion is that universal conscription for a year of national service can be defended on grounds of education as well as of national need. All should go, men and women, for twelve months sometime between their fifteenth and twenty-first birthdays. There should be options, some programs government-run, others privately run with government blessing. The army, hospital work, teaching, conservation work, jobs in prisons and in slums, assistantships in publicly significant research or experimental programs, counseling jobs with youth groups, aides in police and fire departments: the possibilities for older youth are endless. The timing of the particular year that an individual would serve could be left to the discretion of the particular boy or girl and the parents. As colleges and high schools have found, many—if not most—youngsters need a sort of moratorium from climbing the ladder to adulthood. On all grounds, a break may be needed; the change can itself be educationally beneficial; and various social causes, from hospitals to the army, can profit from it.

At the heart of any child's development, whether of power, or of agency, or of joy, is the family. Historical and contemporary evidence overwhelmingly tells us that children from desperate home situations can rarely learn anything not directly concerned with their own simple survival: hungry and ill-clad children are not efficient learners; fearful, badgered children give little trust to those who would teach them. Desperate people nurture their children with difficulty. If most of the family's energy must be focused on survival today, there is rarely any energy for tomorrow's concerns—and a child's education is largely concerned with tomorrow. Moreover, a parent who himself or herself has limited knowledge and little hope can rarely help a child, and indeed may hinder him. Despondency and hopelessness are communicable diseases.

The reinforcement and assistance of the American family is an educational priority of the highest order. Children and their parents should *know* that they will not go hungry and without adequate clothing, housing, or essential utilities. Those who say that such responsibilities rest not with the state but with the family's breadwinner ignore the rights of that breadwinner's child: it is not his fault if Dad or Mom is unemployed, unemployable, slothful, ill, or economically incompetent. At least as long as there is a dependent child in a household, society for his benefit should assure that family a freedom from fear and from hunger, cold, and disease.

But there is more to family security than food, clothing, and shelter. The attitude of parents is important; their own sense of agency will greatly affect their child's. If they have control of some resources (even if these are provided as welfare by the state), they have a certain control over what they do, what they eat, what they wear, where they live. If the options rest exclusively with the state, the not-so-subtle insult to the parents inevitably infects the child. He must live with persons from whom the world has taken even the choices affecting their own offspring. Whether or not the situation is merited is not the point: the child has a right to a parent or parents who have been trusted to make certain decisions about his welfare. Three well-balanced meals offered daily to children in a school cafeteria may be nutritionally sound, but they will certainly undermine the self-respect of most mothers and fathers. One must balance a concern for the physical well-being of a child with a concern for his emotional well-being within a family. And a family without some autonomy is sick.

This line of argument has been repeatedly advanced in recent years. It is at the core of President Nixon's plan for "family assistance." Few attack its basic logic as an efficient approach to welfare. However, few argue for it on educational grounds, and its educational merits have not been promoted by the professional education fraternity. A financial floor under every family of young children also constitutes a kind of educational floor. Hungry, ill-clad, sick, and fearful children can learn little but tactics of survival. They have no energy left to look to the future.

The fear of not having enough money is, of course, only one kind of fear a family may have, but it is one that society can do something about. Families in other kinds of difficulties have a right to counseling; more will be said on this shortly. Along more traditional educational lines, however, all parents should be aware of the steps they can take to assist the rapid and happy development of their young children. There has been made great emphasis in the past on sound physical and emotional development, and properly so; but not nearly enough has been made of intellectual development. As several psycholinguists and educators, such as Basil Bernstein, Roger Brown, and Courtney Cazden, have suggested, a home where a mother helps a child to learn and use rich and varied language advances him materially toward more sophisticated skills of communication and reading.[4] A child from a low-income background is often classified as an academic underachiever as the result of being raised in a language-poor household. As a toddler beginning to talk, he learned only a limited vocabulary, with few subtleties of meaning. This put him at a disadvantage when he started school, and he fell further and further behind, discouraged in school and with little linguistic help at home.

Without a moderate command of language, few children can move either into abstract studies or into modes of communication that the society, not surprisingly, requires for "making it." But as Professors Cazden and Bernstein have demonstrated, women of limited means and education can be trained to broaden their own and their children's vocabularies, thus making their homes much more language-rich. And the child from a low-income family who has language skills can readily achieve as well as the socially more favored youngster, as studies of poor Jewish and Chinese immigrants suggest. If it is at all possible, then, language training should be available to—and urged upon—mothers with limited education. The proper preparation of one mother of five might well be more effective, and far less expensive, than the

4. See, for example, Courtney Cazden's forthcoming book, *Child Language and Education* (New York, 1972).

remedial teaching of each of her youngsters after they enter school.

It seems almost banal to mention that a great deal of good can come of urging mothers to play with (that is, teach) their small children. Yet many mothers do not self-consciously play with their children, or at least miss opportunities to use what interests a child in play to expand his understanding. Many mothers use television merely as a baby-sitter: put Johnny in front of it and leave him be. Yet television, at its best, can be the springboard for all kinds of intellectual exploration. As the producers of *Sesame Street* have discovered, the smaller children who watch the program along with their parents and older sisters and brothers, and who carry on its language and ideas in talk and play afterwards, progress at a rate significantly ahead of children denied these opportunities. The give and take in a home is, of course, a child's whole environment, his own "school" as it were. The more lively it is, the more he may absorb and take interest in. Jibbering to himself or to other little children is not for him as helpful as talking and playing with older youngsters and parents, and their involvement in something which intrigues him—such as a clever routine from *Sesame Street*—is especially enlivening.

In addition, if there are toys and books and materials that relate to a *Sesame Street*, and to the whole family's interest in it, so much the better. A combination of mother-training, television programming, and related books and materials can greatly enrich any home, but especially those which are language-poor and provide few opportunities for a child to visit new places and associate with many different people. Here is one way the society can do something about educationally disadvantaged households, something beyond day-care centers—"alternative homes," as it were, the costs of which may well limit their accessibility to the fee-paying middle class. Virtually every home in the United States has a television set; each one is on for an average of more than fifty hours a week. On the whole, the poorer the family, the more it watches television. And most mothers want to help their children and would take eagerly to learning skills that would make it possible to do so, for they would all certainly make use of toys and books. Very little social pressure would be needed to compel parents to help their offspring; even if one thought such compulsion was moral, it would be largely unnecessary.

In this context, the question comes up: how to define "family"? Mother and children? Mother and father and children? Those who live in a household irrespective of blood relationship? Those of blood relationship living in a particular household? The last seems clearly preferable. It is politic (most Americans are not prepared to recognize a family group that does not give a particular mother definite responsibility for her own children) and yet realistic (it includes the stereotyped, two-generation family of Mom, Dad, Sis, and Bud, but it also includes a more extended household of grandparents, aunts, uncles, and cousins as well as parents, or a conventional family unit within a larger, unrelated community). At the very least is is reasonable for society to expect a mother to be responsible for her child; society should then assist the mother to provide for that child. What kind of larger family unit the mother and child wish to join is none of our business.

There are those who feel that the welfare of every child is a concern of the community as a whole, and that the child's mother and father have no more obligation to it than does anyone else. (Or, put alternatively, all of us have full parental responsibility for every child.) This view ignores the simple fact of mother love. Whether it is socially or biologically induced is beside the point: it exists for the majority of Americans. For any other adult to have responsibility, and thus authority, over their children is something few mothers would be prepared to accept. The mother-child unit is an American sine qua non. Fathers, as they say, are nice; but the presence of the father, while making good sense psychologically, is not for the state to require. The state, on the other hand, should certainly not make it difficult or costly for the father to be at home, as some state-aid programs for children have in effect done; or, when appropriate, for the father to take primary responsibility for the child. Aid, under some statutes, is now given only to fatherless homes; if the father is unemployed, or otherwise unable to support his family, that family is eligible for welfare aid if he is physically absent from the household, if he legally abandons it. State programs should encourage the family to stay together, not assist in disrupting it.

Most contemporary high schools maintain guidance services. But guidance departments have a cluster of responsibilities—psychological testing, personal and vocational counseling, and, sometimes, the discipline of unruly students. And they serve only those who are enrolled in school; comparable services for those beyond school age or for school dropouts are rarely available anywhere. Inevitably, psychological testing will be a task of the academy. Discipline is everyone's job (including that of the children, the apparent objects of discipline), all the time. Passing that buck is an old school game; and the task of the school's special "cop," whether guidance counselor or, more commonly, assistant principal, is an odious one. Personal and vocational counseling are inextricably related and are needed, legitimately, by people at different stages of life.

Why is guidance, then, restricted to the schools? Why isn't it an independent, public concern, available to everyone? What's more, its purpose is not literally *guidance*: the purpose is not to clip a leash on people and lead them along; it is rather to make them confidently autonomous and responsible. And it is not "mental health" in the clinical psychological or psychiatric sense. Every community needs mental health services to treat so-called sick people and to try to prevent recurring illness. These services are essentially medical. Guidance deals with well people (insofar as that distinction holds) and can be directly concerned with the overall social climate in a community. And it need not deal only with individuals: a guidance officer might properly take the initiative to rid a community of a harmful condition—a gang that terrorizes youngsters, for example—rather than simply console the victims of the gang.

As the heart of such service is psychological—a concern for human development apart from physical health—a practitioner could appropriately be called a "public psychologist." His tasks would be dual: to counsel individuals and groups in the best guidance tradition, and to be an advocate and catalyst for the improvement of community conditions. We have watchdogs for sanitary abuses, watchdogs for pollution; we should have watchdogs for psychological harassment as well.

A lively example of the use of public psychology was Boston's Playroom 81, on Mission Hill. Three professionals—a clinical psychologist, an educator, and a community leader—served as catalysts for the creation of a racially integrated day-care center in a tense housing project. The staff helped fight city hall, wrote proposals for funding, and gave advice; but they saw to it that the enterprise was led, essentially, by a group of concerned mothers. The staff, by encouraging these women, most of whom were on welfare, persuaded them that they could create and run a center, something they desperately wanted for their children. In a direct way, these mothers were helped to a deep sense of agency.[5]

An interesting experiment in the use of a computer to "teach" vocational decision-making has been conducted by David V. Tiedeman and his colleagues. Tiedeman devised a series of programmed exercises to assist an individual to discriminate among job opportunities, requirements, and rewards, and he set up these games to be "played" with

5. Robert Belenky, "School Psychology and Community Organization: The Playroom 81 Model," *Occasional Paper No. 2 of the Harvard University Center for Research and Development on Educational Differences* (Cambridge, 1967).

current labor-market data. That is, an individual would learn about career choice—about the kinds of questions a person should reasonably have regarding an employment possibility—from a series of problems drawn from the existing labor situation. This "information system for vocational decisions," as Tiedeman called it, can be used wherever a console connected to a computer can be maintained. It is a good example of an autonomous counseling system, though the current costs of operation make it uneconomic with today's technology.[6]

The guidance or counseling function that is now performed in schools, while clearly part of education, should be independent, tied not to schools, or to mental-health centers, or hospitals, or city hall. Practically speaking, most public psychologists would be laymen—trained by professionals. The enterprise's main purpose would be to make every man sensitive and aware, every man himself a counselor.

A softheaded mirage? Not if the idea is kept practical, resisting the usual guild instinct to require that all services be rendered exclusively by professionals: the point is to help ordinary people themselves to provide guidance. Not if public psychology stays away from the medical imagery of sick and well people, with services provided exclusively for the former: the point of public psychology is to ameliorate the conditions that lead to psychological misery in a community and to help individuals where they are, whether or not they are clinically ill or healthy. Not if public psychologists give careful thought to the scale of their efforts, selecting enterprises that promise reasonable payoffs for a significant number of people. The all too common professional tendency is for a psychologist to drift into intense involvement with a few, interesting individuals; these rapidly become clients and the public psychologist becomes a full-time therapist. This one-to-one work is satisfying and hassle-free; and the more complicated, community-wide concerns that

6. See *Annual Reports of the Information System for Vocational Decisions* (Harvard Graduate School of Education, 1966-1969).

affect the spirits of many people are invariably neglected. In short, the specialized guidance functions now provided in schools should be recast, broadened, and organized along autonomous lines to serve entire communities, not just those people who happen to be attending school.

How to meet the ends of joy? It is easier to prescribe for power and agency. That aspect of joy which can be called appreciation is an aspect of power, for discrimination is at its heart. Appreciation requires diverse experience: one develops taste only through exposure to a succession of contrasts. Variety in the media is essential here. Imagine a kind of *Civilisation* series prepared by Andy Warhol. And more.

Sensitivity is an obvious goal of the collegium and can be provided for. However, it is the freedom aspect of joy which is the rub: by definition alone, the experience of liberation cannot be a subject of corporate planning; it cannot be "provided for." Its destructive aspects—the freedom of a Charles Manson cult—clearly must be checked; but within these obvious and extreme limits, the stance of most Americans must be one of tolerance. Social experiment is as important as scientific experiment, and often just as risky. The communal family is hardly as dangerous an experiment as the hydrogen bomb (though perhaps more socially influential, in the long run), yet we pillory those who engage in the former and honor those instrumental in the latter. We should respect social and scientific experiment—and reserve the right to examine each closely and criticize severely. We cannot accept the arrogant "you-just-don't-understand" rebuttal from either nuclear physicist or practical utopian. In sum, the process of liberation—experiments in extending human joy—must be encouraged, but we will continue to question and criticize. Such a policy makes obvious good sense, yet we are failing miserably to practice it. We give public financial support to the spiritual agencies of the majority of Americans (through tax waivers for churches), but we have no room for serious hippies. Most Americans insist that their particular version of joy is the only respectable joy. But personal commitments of all kinds (except for those which, clearly and wrongfully, injure others) deserve not only tolerance but protection. A child has a right to spiritual commitment and the experiments that lead to it. He must have warning and the counsel of adults, of course, and information on practices that can harm him (what the excessive use of drugs or alcohol can do, for example); but he has the moral right to be himself. This is part of education and can be defended politically on those grounds.

No single institution can provide all of a child's education. Many institutions teach, in varied, powerful ways. A sensible educational policy would loosely ally a cluster of these, their combination becoming the total school. Family, academy, collegium, the communications media, work, the larger community—all teach, and all can be assisted powerfully in the child's best interests.

Inevitably, the aims of education encompass a cluster of dilemmas, the child's goals clashing with the interests of corporate society. There is no single moral accommodation to these: all we can do is assure the child the powers of discrimination. Better than imposed accommodation is a diversity of schools, with exposure to many different values. Out of such diversity, and with discrimination, a child can find a just and personally satisfying place in society.

5

Means

How to change "the system"?

Given the satisfaction most Americans have with present arrangements, reform will be difficult. For a start, however, the country could benefit from some straightforward facts— facts about what we are doing, what appears to serve children well and what doesn't. The delusions upon which much of current satisfaction rests must be exposed, and the greater effectiveness of some alternatives to our present way of educating youngsters clearly demonstrated. Such will require study, that popularly misunderstood enterprise called "research."

Today, the justification of our work in schools rests upon a mixture of common sense and science. The latter needs expansion at the expense of the former, which is more often than not now either unintentional prejudice or unexamined tradition. Of course, much of education will inevitably remain a matter of values, rather than of measurable technique. Whether the schools should or should not be used as vehicles for social reform, such as interracial harmony, is a matter primarily of political belief and only secondarily of execution. But there is much in education that is susceptible to organized inquiry, to scientific illumination.

The questions to ask are obvious. How do individuals, inevitably of differing backgrounds, learn? Conversely, how can certain subject matters be presented so that they can be learned? Such questions are easy to state, but extremely difficult to solve. An enormous diversity among people and among kinds of learning has to be accommodated. Take one important social topic, an individual's perceptions of other racial groups: how are these perceptions now formed? Do individual members of differing cultural, economic, and racial groups "learn" to perceive others in different ways? How do one's perceptions alter as one grows older? Which factors outside of the family—for example, neighborhood, school, television—appear to be most powerful in shaping those perceptions? Conversely, if one wishes individuals to be aware, generous, and tolerant of groups other than their own, how is this best accomplished? Mixing groups? Social studies teaching? Political action that encourages hostile groups to see more clearly their common purposes? Related to both these approaches are fundamental philosophical problems. How may one define a man's perception of another? Assuming that the society has the capability of shaping attitudes (through the media or compulsory education, for example), can nationally *imposed* perceptions be justified by the social stability that may accrue from lessened hostility among races? Or does an individual have a right to hate, and, if so, under what constraints?

There are other kinds of examples, some humble. How do children from different backgrounds learn to write? What part does physiology (that is, the ability to manipulate a pencil) play in shaping a person's expression? What are the connections between what a person thinks and what he writes? What appears to shape the style of a person's writing? Conversely, given a definition of a form of exposition, how can it best be taught? What pedagogical accommodations must be made to factors of age, social class, or cultural group? And again there are philosophical questions. At what points do social priorities (for example, for people who can write sensible and legible prose) impinge on individual priorities (for example, to write in a mode which the current society may find opaque, but which may reach to new, if yet unappreciated, forms of expression)?

To repeat: the questions are obvious. There is nothing that the layman will find incomprehensible in the purposes of educational research. But its execution is enormously difficult, and, while much has been done, it is only a beginning. The key questions, while obvious, are complex, having many interrelated parts. To understand them, one needs to cut across several of the academic disciplines. They require *time* for solution, not only to allow for the unraveling of their complexity, but also to permit the study of individuals over time. Most learning is, probably, a process of growth; if one wishes to understand that process, one must track that growth over time. There are few instant answers in education. In addition, scientific inquiry requires courage, as many findings are sure to affront convictions. The fact that schools do not accomplish what we currently assert they do is difficult to accept. The fact that genetics almost surely has some effect on educability will inevitably be resisted, probably with a vehemence reminiscent of William Jennings Bryan. Understanding of the biochemistry of learning will lead to possibilities for the use of drugs to forward education: this will appall some (even as they pop aspirin). The revolutionary implications of an education that develops a truly critical intellect will be unpopular with the powers that be at any given time. But responsible change will only emerge from new understanding, however unpopular. If the research supporting that new understanding is sound, reforms will eventually follow.

A first step in improving education is, then, to learn more about the process of learning and then to apply it. Such is logical, but not, to date, politically obvious. This country spends less than one percent of its operating funds for public education on either fundamental inquiry or even evaluation of what is currently happening. The private educational sector spends proportionally even less; its claim for experiment and excellence rests largely upon snobbish rhetoric. Most Americans will have to be persuaded that they need to know more about education; they must be cajoled to see how little of the current enterprise rests on solid evidence. While exposure of our inadequacies will inevitably aid the mindless budget cutters who infect any culture, it also can, if sensibly argued, aid those who want to press forward with useful research and experiment—and, eventually, sound reform.[1]

Exposure of difficulties and failures alone, however, is largely destructive, and the successes and wisdom in American educational tradition need illumination and explication as well. As has been argued in chapter two, the general expectations of most Americans about the ends of education—power, agency, and joy—are both progressive and useful. However precisely defined, they serve as a basis for public consideration of the detailed purposes of education, a process which must precede any rational rearrangement of the system. The national press is the principal agency to forward this discussion, and, while the reporting of widely held beliefs is rarely the kind of news which sells papers and magazines, it can be done imaginatively. Consideration could well start from an effort at translating these purposes into specific forms—the technique employed in this book, of course, in chapters three and four—and then work back onto fundamental questions of purpose. Only sharply focused issues catch public interest; specificity is essential. The material is there in abundance, waiting for a journalist-interpreter, or a schoolman's Ralph Nader.

Obviously, educators themselves must rid their profession of delusory icons. Myopia and confusion are forgivable in the general public, but intolerable in a group that is supposed to

1. See Lee J. Cronbach and Patrick Suppes, *Research for Tomorrow's Schools: Disciplined Inquiry for Education* (New York, 1969).

lead its field. The steps to be taken here are quite simple: broaden the view of Faculties of Education by employing there more professors who are well trained in research and familiar with broad social issues, and concentrate university training on the relatively small corps of individuals who are actually leading the system, the "master" teachers and policy makers.

Such sounds easy in theory, but will be difficult in practice. "Research," for many in Education, means counting up things and "analyzing" them, inquiring how many principals in six counties in the eastern part of the state "like" French taught in the sixth grade and then drawing "conclusions" from this survey. Due to the complexity of education, inquiry into its functions requires special imagination and skill, and, given the wide range of settings, including schools, in which children learn, sophisticated scholarly breadth is essential. A first-class corps of investigators must be found, as there are lamentably few first-class scholars at work today.

Training raises different kinds of problems. The initial (preservice) training of teachers which now absorbs most of the energy and imagination of professors of education should be sharpened, with "craft" training—in actual teaching—carried out in training centers within schools. Liberal studies, as now, would be pursued primarily in Arts faculties. Theoretical work of high and significant quality in education—something relatively rare today, given the narrow training and perspective of many professors in the field—should be at a minimum for neophytes and at a maximum for the able careerist, that one individual among the many who entered teaching who has chosen to stay with it, who is effective at it, comfortable and successful with children, and competent to look at education as more than merely a mechanical problem of classroom management. This careerist is crucial: he shapes schools and he influences young teachers. Change his view and understanding, and the schools will, in time, be profoundly affected. Such happened in English primary schools over the last forty years; it can happen in the United States as well. Professionals can, given time, lead the system.

The professional *cursus honorum* would, then, emerge as follows: a liberal arts course toward a bachelor's degree; supervised experience in the craft of teaching toward the end of undergraduate study or after it, with seminars on pedagogy offered in the schools; paid teaching (the first years with minimal supervision and help, as needed); and, finally, periodic return to the university by those who will devote most of their lives to teaching, there to pursue theoretical study and careful examination of their craft and the institutions in which it is practiced. The schools will require special staffs to conduct this preservice training: it cannot be done by any teacher in addition to his normal duties. It would be best carried out by a team of teachers, working out of a school's or a school system's curriculum resources center, a place where all teachers could come to develop teaching materials and swap ideas about their craft. Such centers are now in existence in many American communities, and in several English counties Teacher Centers have become highly influential and obviously useful. What better setting to induct newcomers into education than among the liveliest teachers gathered to reconsider and improve their work?

The focus in these centers would properly be on the pedagogical craft; and the craft necessarily implies the existence of relatively stable schools, with teachers and children and curriculum fixed within generally accepted parameters. Theoretical study and the field experiments of universities, in contrast, would *not* assume institutional stability, and would (as all good research must) challenge the very basis and conduct of the craft. The careerist educator must both be a master of his craft and a highly skilled critic of it. While all crafts need their critics, this is especially true in education, where so much evidence abounds to challenge the status quo. Universities must forward this challenge, must be places of skepticism, challenging even the best of the craft. Traditionally, the colleges have not been, preferring the comfort of mutual admiration with schoolmen. Even those who would reform schools have tried the unwise wedding of craftsman and skeptic: the United States Office of Education in the 1960's preached often on how the researcher had to be given his problem for study by the practitioner. Listen to the teachers, it was said; they'll tell you what needs fixing. The place of academic theory and revolutionary scholarship was completely misunderstood; the craft was expected to delineate the areas for study. Basic research in learning and in the influences of a variety of educating institutions, albeit including the schools, appeared to have no place. The urge to make research "practical" was an ironically conservative step. Inquiry wedded to even the best of the craft does not allow for fundamental skepticism about the system itself.

The schools should forward the craft of teaching, and the universities the means of understanding it and constructively reconstruing it. For practical reasons, the schools should train the novices. The universities should concentrate on the education of the careerists. In so doing, the quality of training will improve—and, likely, savings of money and students' time also be made.

The profession, thus, can play a part in reform, but its approach will take time—changing teachers' styles and attitudes does not happen quickly. On the other hand, politics can alter the structure of education relatively quickly. Politics itself also informs laymen and professionals alike. When Governor William Milliken of Michigan suggested that state government assume responsibility for all school finance, he provoked a rumble of debate, much of it very much to the point, as he was challenging the myth of localism. The politician who attacks the icons will find that the risks are high: School is Mom. Yet if he picks the most blatant failures (such as the fact that many teenaged school children can't even read) or the most abrasive issues (such as the bankruptcy of many municipal budgets), he has, if he persists, a chance to gain political mileage. Lyndon Johnson used educational issues well. The work of his administration and that of the 89th Congress changed irreversibly and, on the whole, wisely the role of the federal government in American schooling. Johnson's lever was, of course, poverty. Persistence is essential. Commissioner of Education James E. Allen, Jr., gave President Nixon a first-class issue with the Right to Read program, but Nixon failed to carry through, and, along with his subsequent firing of Allen, provoked only hostility from those who were concerned with schools. Milliken of Michigan is gaining support for his "full-state-funding" notion; state and federal courts are challenging both the ability of current fiscal policies to guarantee equal expenditures for education across each state (through a challenge of the local property tax, the primary source of school revenue) and the inviolability of school district lines (through a challenge of such lines as vehicles for de facto class and race discrimination). Respected reformers such as James Conant are calling now not only for full state funding but also for state-level teacher salary and benefit negotiations. Conant specifically rejects his 1950's "local control" stance.[2]

If each child is to have roughly the same numbers of dollars spent on his education as every other child, central governments will have inevitably to collect and distribute tax revenues. Such a bold assertion is an example of how White House or state house or legislature or state and federal courts can provoke the public to rethink what its schools stand for and how well they are working. Few bold proposals succeed at first, as attitudes take time to change. But only a decade passed between Eisenhower's first White House Conference on Education—which was adamant to limit a federal role in education—and the Elementary and Secondary Education

2. James B. Conant, in the 1972 Alfred Dexter Simpson Lecture, New England School Development Council.

Act of 1965, which brought Washington directly and massively into the schools. The ESEA is itself only a beginning. Like many prototype laws, it is a flimsy structure of compromises between cities, states, professional lobbies, and organized religious bodies. Its function as a myth smasher (central government *can* play a sensible role in schools, and the church-state issue *is* negotiable) and as a provocation to debate (such as that emerging from the asserted failure of Title I's programs for poor children) is obvious.

Politics can raise issues long buried. Government can, of course, reform the system more directly by a careful shuffling of money: the dollar is a prime mover of institutions. Those who would use it must understand the influence of finance on the workings of the system, as the allocation of money has political and pedagogical side effects. For example, if homogeneity, consistency, and close political control are particularly desired, a public authority should operate the schools. It should decide how the moneys are spent, and the client—the child—offered a service. If diversity is a primary end, moneys should be given directly to the client (or his parents), who then can select the service he desires and pay for it directly. The former practice, of course, is the rule in American elementary and secondary education (though not in higher education where various aid schemes, most notably the so-called G.I. Bill of Rights, support students with direct, personal grants and allow them to select their own programs at approved institutions). Various kinds of "education voucher" schemes, examples of the latter practice, have recently been proposed for schools. Many are justified as devices to improve schools by making them competitive, to create, simply, a marketplace for education. Schools which satisfy customers will survive; those that do not will cease to exist. The assumptions are that parents' judgment of how well a school succeeds is no worse than that of anyone else, and perhaps better (the principal axe most parents have to grind is the most relevant possible one: whether their child is learning anything important), and that the system can be distinctly improved by the process of competition for parents' favor. Most serious advocates of voucher plans realize that such a marketplace could not be entirely free, and some, such as Christopher Jencks, have proposed elaborate new political entities ("education voucher authorities," in his words) to supervise the system.[3] Some plans—again Jencks's is a good example—are radical, calling for all state, local, and federal school moneys to be pooled and divided into vouchers. Other schemes would have vouchers employed solely by the federal government, in support of compensatory education for poor children in addition to existing local and state arrangements.[4] These compensatory voucher schemes have far fewer political liabilities than a total scheme, such as Jencks's, but they would likely provoke only minimal competition among schools. Their purpose is less to create a marketplace than both to give a low-income youngster's parents greater control over his education and to bestow on that child a kind of financial "attractiveness" to schools competing for his attendance. (A poor child's voucher could materially assist a school's budget; the more poor children a school had, the richer its programs could be; accordingly, poor children would be sought after, even by schools with middle-class student bodies. Class—and racial—integration in classrooms might thus be significantly increased.)

Diversity is unlikely if resources are controlled by a single authority. Homogeneity and common standards are unlikely if resources are spread widely, with individual clients calling the tune. Unchallenged, unitary authorities are likely to become rigid and unresponsive. A system that depends on the sale of wares can easily become faddist and susceptible to the

3. Christopher S. Jencks, *Educational Vouchers: A Report on Financing Elementary Education by Grants to Parents* (Cambridge, Mass., 1970).
4. Theodore R. Sizer and Phillip Whitten, "A Proposal for a Poor Children's Bill of Rights," *Psychology Today* (August 1968), p. 58.

huckster. Given the concurrent need of American education to provide, at a minimum, for some *common* standards (of power) and for *varied and diverse* experience (for agency), *a mix of direct and indirect funding is likely to be required.* Such can be accomplished in the current political climate, as a mix inevitably has something for everyone. Altering school funding *patterns* (even more than funding levels) is a task readily achievable in the current political climate.

More difficult (as Governor Milliken and the courts are finding) will be the assault on the local control of education. While most academic decisions affecting individual children should be left, even more than at present, to individual academies and collegia (of which more later), the substantial, across-the-board authority now held by some 20,000 autonomous school authorities must be sharply curtailed. The argument that the strength of American education is found in its localism is a myth, and continued belief in it will stifle reform. Localism has not created diversity: American schools are strikingly alike in curriculum, style, even in teachers' jargon. (The significant differences which lead to varying performance of schools are not to be found in the schools' design and practice but in the social class composition of student bodies.) There may be many school districts, but they are under little compulsion to compete with one another. We have, in essence, some 20,000 monopoly situations. Furthermore, the level of government which raises the money for the operation of schools should have ultimate authority over it, and local communities will, hopefully and perhaps inevitably, have a decreasing role in tax collection. An authority which must raise revenues for someone else's disbursement rarely raises them with zeal; and authorities which spend someone else's money often lack painstaking concern for its proper management. Few localities, even large cities, can squeeze the property and local sales tax any further. The federal government and the states have broader and more effective revenue-raising abilities, and they will inevitably—irrespective of the final practical outcome of the challenges to the local property tax, such as *Serrano v. Priest*—have to carry an even greater share of school operating costs. (Several states, such as Delaware, Hawaii, and to a lesser extent several southeastern states, carry the lion's share of the burden already.) Accordingly, it is prudent that they take a greater share in the management of education. This can be accomplished, it should be stressed, without creating a centralized and highly standardized curriculum.

There are other equally telling arguments against localism. The extraordinary mobility of the population means that any community rarely educates for itself: its children end up in other locales. The neighborhood school is not the cradle of its village, but rather a service provided for the children of families passing through. An adult who was inadequately schooled in community A ends up as a burden, perhaps unemployable, for community B. Simple equity among American communities would suggest that some significant general responsibility for minimal standards be available.

Furthermore, as *Serrano* tellingly demonstrates, some wealthy communities can support more elaborate schools than can their poorer counterparts. Some states provide more lavishly for their education than others. These inequities are hardly the fault of the children, and some national and regional equity of investment in their education is a clear necessity. Rich areas will have to help support poor schools: it is as simple (and likely to be as politically unpopular) as that.

Finally, there is the problem of a locality's breadth, of its variety. A true community is, after all, a group of people with similar values. A child should learn those values, at home and, too, at school; but he should also be exposed to other values. We all applaud community control when we happen to like the values of that community. The civil rights activist supports a black neighborhood's seizure of its schools, arguing that that "village" needs a place it can itself

oversee, one staffed with its servants, not those hired by a
"foreign" majoritarian group. But when a beleaguered,
Wallace-ite community takes the same position, our activist is
on the other side. The only resolution is to insist that all
children are taught to think clearly (which is difficult
enough), and that all children have a *variety* of educational
experience. It is not enough to grow up in only one milieu,
however perfect that may appear to be. A child must have
the experience of learning in several communities, many with
differing points of view. No level of government can or
should try to enforce any one value, save that of justice. But
a child who is raised in only a single set of values is its
prisoner, most often unwittingly. Government can at least
assure that a child has varied experience, chances to see
beyond his village.

These are straightforward arguments, but sure to provoke
passionate opposition. Only a financial crisis will temper this
passion, and that crisis, happily, is upon us. Those responsible
for reshaping the fiscal system for American education have a
rare opportunity to reassert state and federal authority in
education, to break the grip of localism and, through a mix
of direct and indirect funding, promise greater diversity to
American education.

At this point, it would be well to be concrete, and to
reconcile the recommendations for multiple schools—
academies and collegia—with those for altered funding and
control. At the heart of these is state government, which
should support unitary, "first" schools for very young children, and multiple systems of academies and collegia for
youngsters beyond the age of ten. Support for the first
schools and for academies should be largely in the form of
direct grants to individual institutions, with supplementary
education vouchers for children both from low-income
homes and with clearly identifiable academic difficulties. The
neighborhoods served by a particular academy should be set

by the state. "Neighborhoods" may not only be narrow geographical entities; the constituency for several academies— to insure that each is not totally class segregated, for example—could be drawn from a single broad region. Each academy should have a governing board drawn from parents (elected) and others (state appointed, a majority from the locale which the academy serves). This board would appoint the principal (subject to state veto) and would review his staff appointments, budget, and program.

Once that centralized state government sponsors an academy, decisions should be largely left in the hands of that school's leadership and clients. The principal should have great autonomy, more analogous to the English than the current American pattern, and his staff should set the curriculum and organize the school. Higher authorities should assist, not direct. The academy should receive a block grant from the state, based on enrollment. For each child from a low-income family (for whom special efforts and extra services may be necessary) and for each youngster clearly behind in academic performance, based on the state's examination (for whom special, remedial teaching would be required), the academy would receive supplementary vouchers from the parents of the children enrolled. The principal would need his board's approval on his annual budget and would submit to a yearly state audit.

What parents legitimately want from a school is accessibility and responsiveness: a state academy, with a principal and board with substantial autonomy, could provide this. While the intellectual objectives of the academy would be relatively precise (certainly relative to today's standards) and its curriculum inevitably influenced by state examinations, considerable local flexibility to accommodate individual children's needs would be attainable.

The teachers would be drawn from those with state certification and would be paid on a salary scale negotiated with the state. There would be several classes of teachers—so-called master teachers, teachers, associate teachers, aides, and interns—which would allow a principal to balance his staff among long-experienced professionals, newcomers, and so forth. As Robert Anderson, Francis Keppel, and others have argued for over two decades, the assumptions that all teachers are of essentially equivalent ability and style and that they should be granted life tenure after but the first three years of teaching are absurd on their very face (but, as with so many things in American education, persist, nonetheless).[5] Some system which well rewards able teachers and only modestly rewards the modestly competent, which allows a child to be taught by a variety of adults, which allows teachers to work where their talents lie (the reading expert on reading, the art expert on art, and so forth) and which relieves skilled teachers from time-wasting, routine details is clearly needed. Teacher tenure would apply only to the level at which an individual was rated: an associate teacher would have no claim to automatic promotion but would have a claim to retention at that rank, save on the occasion of gross incompetence or immorality. The state, through a professional standards board, comprised to a significant degree of teachers themselves, would administer teacher rating, which would be based largely on performance, not on collected credits in graduate courses, or in mere time served. The state would have the right to inspect the academy regularly, and the state board of education could order it closed if conditions warranted. The governing board would be informed of the progress of pupils on the state examination program.

The state could entertain proposals for a variety of academies serving a particular region. While a governing board would have responsibility for each, it might choose to contract the operation of the school to a private company, or to a team of teachers organized together expressly for that purpose. Physical facilities would be the property of the state, however; and, likewise, the state would underwrite capital building.

5. See, for example, Francis Keppel, *Personnel Policies for Public Education* (Pittsburgh, 1961).

A child would be compelled to attend an academy at least
fifteen hours a week during the traditional school year, until
he was fifteen, or for an additional period either if he had
failed the state's simple tests for power, or if he simply
wished to do so. (In the latter case, he could pay for such
experience with the vouchers given him for enrollment in
collegia; in the former, the state would continue to finance
his education by direct capitation grants to an academy.)

The idea of a uniform, minimal test of power—of the
ability to discriminate abstractly and to perform simple
communication skills—will horrify most Americans. A national exam, leading to centralized thought control? An American version of the notorious, British Eleven-Plus exam, or the
French Baccalaureat? A clever device to keep minorities
down with a kind of generalized literacy test? Such fears are
fair ones, and must be addressed. There need not be *one* test:
power discrimination can be assessed in a variety of ways;
there can be a variety of measures. The tests need not be
entirely written, formal examinations, but a series of exercises, some judged subjectively by teachers. The tests need
not be set by government, but by an autonomous, govern-
ment-sponsored body, staffed by experts. The tests would be
of skills, not of values (insofar as this is possible); of
systematic judgment, not of belief; of process, primarily,
rather than of the "coverage" of a "subject." They can be
seen not as barriers, but as checkpoints for the benefit of the
student: a child who fails gets *more* help until he succeeds.
Failure provokes assistance, then, not rejection or exclusion.

It will be difficult for many Americans to take seriously the
point that academic schooling does have assessable content,
some of which is systematic and thus measurable. (Some,
too, will also have difficulty in remembering that part of
education is *not* systematic, and thus not practically measurable.) The public must see that a child without minimal—very
minimal—skills of language, and numbers, and logic is a
crippled child. It is an immoral society which fails to lessen

its numbers of cripples or the extent of their affliction. Americans must realize that most children—the overwhelming majority—*can* learn, if only the effort is made, and if only people believe in those children. In a word, we should not give up on any youngster, however dull, or hostile, or distant he appears to be. A minimum level of power should be seen as a kind of national promise: this is a floor below which no child should be effortlessly allowed to fall.

Given their authority for education, the states should be responsible for making available tests of power. A child—or adult—could take them at any time or place and as many times as he wishes. Some eight-year-olds will exceed the minimum standard; some sixteen-year-olds will fall below it. Any child who has obvious difficulty at a test, or at the work leading to it, should have special support. No child with even the remotest chance of successfully passing it should be denied help to do so.

At the same time, the diverse experience required for achieving a sense of agency would be provided in collegia for children from the age of ten, as previously argued. A child would, by current standards, attend an academy only part-time, and the rest of his effort would be spent in one or more of the activities that primarily promote agency. Each child, irrespective of income, would receive vouchers "cashable" at accredited collegia, or, in special cases for youngsters and adults over the age of fifteen, at academies. The vouchers would be good for a person's entire life (indeed, they form the basis of a sane approach to further adult education, an important topic beyond the scope of this book). Save for the system of national service, which would be federally financed, sponsored, and administered, accreditation would be the responsibility of the states but could be delegated to appointed regional boards, separate from those for any academy and comprised of both laymen and educators. A collegium would be judged on its program alone. Its staff would not have to be certified, as with academy teachers, nor would the collegium have to be "substantial" (for example, two able young outdoorsmen who run wilderness trips for small groups of boys and girls could comprise a collegium). Academies could themselves sponsor collegia. A regional board would require staff to review proposals for collegia and to visit them and would periodically publish reports on the virtues and demerits of each enterprise. The board would also have funds to provide for counseling for parents and children, either organized as an adjunct of regional public psychology services or, less happily, as a branch of an academy. The criteria that a board would use to accredit a collegium would be difficult indeed to devise, and would, in the last analysis, depend on wise, subjective judgments. Collegia at the least would be subject to civil rights laws. As the regional boards would be drawn from several constituencies, no one ideology would likely emerge. Radical enterprises, of whatever merit, would probably not gain accreditation: few politically balanced boards would allow it. But moderate experiments could well gain accreditation and financial support through their clients' vouchers. The boards would also want to monitor student choices; if groups of youngsters picked from a narrow set of collegia, the board might want to urge, through their counseling staff, more variety on parents.

While the states' concerns are clearly for formal education, stimulation and improvement of education outside of formal academies and collegia is a clear federal responsibility. Certainly the intentions of the Public Television Act of 1970 need to be acted upon, and its programs fully funded. Development costs of programs such as *Sesame Street* should be publicly underwritten and, in districts yet unserved by public television, time on commercial channels purchased.

State and federal government can properly give tax advantages (or the flip side of that coin, direct grants) to businesses which provide high-quality, vocationally oriented training outside of collegia. This practice is one that goes back, in important respects, to the Smith-Hughes Act of 1918. What is needed here is an improvement in quality, and a new concern for job training that prepares young people to accommodate to a rapidly changing job market.

The support of research and experiment is clearly both a state and federal responsibility, and, also, one of private foundations. The support must, for reasons expressed earlier, be sustained, allowing sufficient time for sound findings to emerge. It will demand far more patience than the federal bureaucracy has heretofore demonstrated in this field. Full-scale experiments—that is, ones involving entire schools or clusters of schools—must be given not only time, but freedom. Schools as bold as England's Summerhill will not result from a committee, or from a program which requires assessable quarterly progress. Most experiments in education are initially acts of faith and demand the focused vision of a single man or a like-minded group. They need time, room, and even protection, as the most interesting experiments are likely to be also the most controversial. Most recent, publicly financed trials have suffered from an excess of doleful critics. The broth was spoiled, or at best watered down, with compromise. All good science requires courage and patience. Educational science is no exception.

6

Beyond Structure

The suggestions for reform outlined in the preceding chapters emerge from an analysis of current public expectations for education. They are presented principally as proposals for structural changes, such as the creation of academies and collegia, the revision of funding policies, and the devising of examinations to foster minimal educational standards for the nation. Being cast in the form of institutional changes, the traditional mode of reform of liberals, they are only marginally threatening: I am not recommending revolution or a fundamental change in life styles here. The recommendations are, in all, politically feasible and professionally practical.

The problem is, of course, that *current* expectations take little account of *future* realities. Mass expectations, insofar as they can ever be identified, rarely do. This is no great weakness when change in the culture evolves slowly. Today's goals fit reasonably well on tomorrow's problems, or so it has seemed. History allows a lag. However, there is much to suggest that our tomorrow is not going to be so kind: Americans are moving with unprecedented speed into new conditions, into strikingly new sets of surroundings. Current expectations will simply not do for the education of children who will be in their twenties in 1985 and in their forties in the year 2000.

Emerging problems, moreover, are not of a character that can be addressed primarily through structure. The traditional American liberal response to problems of changing institutions will succeed less and less, for the issues are not ones of arrangement but of attitude, not ones of social organization but of social interaction. Changing the structure without changing the individuals who constitute that structure is every day more and more ineffective. Men's minds make the difference, not the governmental and social institutions imposed upon them. Of course, our hope is that deliberately altered structures will become vehicles for altering men's prejudices—racially integrated schools are an example of that hope. But such instances are rare, and even when they exist, they are not supported on the grounds that they will change people's attitudes. Black children and white children go to the same schools because separate schools are inherently unequal, we assert, not because blacks and whites have to learn to be less bigoted. We assume that people are static and that the best we can do is to manipulate the market, or the policy, or the surroundings. Corporately we do not consider the possibility of *changing the people* rather than their institutions. This is not as though the public is not being changed all the time—it gave up Kolynos for Crest, and learned to believe that all Communists are "bad," the friendship with the Soviet Union during World War II to the contrary notwithstanding. But neither politicians nor educators dare to articulate a goal in terms of altering the behavior of individuals: a people less bigoted, or more discriminating, or more compassionate. If such an end is identified at all, it is quickly delegated to the churches. Bigotry and compassion are aspects of religion, it appears; and it would be impolitic to suggest that the American public is not now discriminating. (It wasn't always this way, of course. Jefferson was determined to create "republican" attitudes, and McGuffey to create moral Horatio Algers.)

Most of the evidence suggests, however, that a free and

humane American society can exist only if there is a change in national attitudes. Individual Americans will have to behave differently toward each other, and toward social problems. Unless they begin to do so, no corporate effort at reform is likely to emerge. The struggle will not be over American institutions but over American minds.

There are abundant instances of the current overemphasis on structure at the expense of attitudes: the economically elegant development plan that fails in practice due to the persistence of tribal hierarchies among the people; the restructured university that brings together for decision-making the old and the young, but falls victim to the patronizing arrogance of the one and the ignorant posturing of the other; the public housing project which takes no account of how people communicate, and what they think is pleasant, salubrious, and essential. Once again, the exceptions are found largely in business enterprises that have used advertising effectively, such as the soap industry. Curiously, when we do recognize the effectiveness of private enterprise in shaping attitudes (such as Vance Packard discusses in *The Hidden Persuaders*), we draw the wrong conclusion and move to restrict those who "package souls" (as Packard puts it) rather than to educate individual citizens to resist the huckster's blandishments.

As the Catholic Church, Madison Avenue, and George Gallup can testify, people's opinions *can* be changed and *do* change. Individuals need to become more discriminating to be able to resist the gulling of advertisers, politicians, and even their closest relatives. But this is essentially a negative virtue, a kind of intellectual armor. What the radically different culture facing us in the near future calls for is a broader, more humane outlook, discriminating yet compassionate.

Writing about the need for public attitudes such as compassion, I can hear the critics guffaw. Can a people really love their neighbors? Can a people learn a modicum of tolerance?

Can they, as individuals within a mass, come to demand facts about issues affecting their lives and the ability to analyze them? My dear fellow, critics will wryly remind, the churches have tried all this for centuries, and even they were quickly corrupted by their hierarchies, feuds, and ritual murders. How can one seriously consider a secular cleansing of public attitudes? Soft-headed utopianism, that's what.

But one must persist because there is no alternative: the future promises a surfeit of difficult change; and without a growth in the autonomous power of individuals, this change will lead to less and less freedom for all. One persists, too, because such cleansings have happened before; there have been crusades which fired men's minds—not only demonic movements that gained momentum through deception, but crusades that labored toward human autonomy, dignity, and charity. (There are few ideal examples: one thinks of the work of several of the early Christians, of some nineteenth-century romantics, of Gandhi, of Martin Luther King. To be fair, we must add some of the early ideology of the Communist revolution, before it, like Christianity, became corrupted by its self-deception.) One does consider the possibility of changing public attitudes: given time and imagination, a discriminating citizenry *can* be created, through education. People can learn power, agency, and joy. It simply takes will, and patience.

Such a belief is full of tricky assumptions, however. One must believe that a more rational society will be a better society, that people who can think for themselves will more often than not choose on the charitable side, that the basis of moral behavior is the intellect, not instinct. One can so believe, for either of two reasons: cynically, because if everyone is discriminating, no individual is likely to forward himself by exclusive selfishness (he will be caught and punished either by the law or, more likely, by the mockery and disdain of his associates); or idealistically, because if people really understood the effects of their behavior, they would be more careful than they now are not to commit antisocial acts. A second assumption is that a condition of meaningful personal autonomy is possible, that society can give an individual room to allow his powers of discrimination to count for something. Are personal initiative and freedom possible? The answer must be, of course, that freedom is a matter of degree; but certainly Americans can be significantly, even decisively, more discriminating than they are now. Still another assumption has to do with effort: are the pressing problems descending upon us best dealt with through a corporate change of will? Or are they best met by a wise elite, quickly, before they overwhelm us? The only answer there is the cliché that democracy is an exceedingly bad form of government but all other forms are worse. The likelihood that a *wise* elite would survive is not very high, as the recent history of newly independent nations seems to suggest. Finally, there is the question of the usefulness of formal education, in view of its current limited success in, for example, counteracting the effects of social class. But education has in the past been so straightjacketed by dysfunctional traditions and so starved of resources that a fair trial has yet to be made.

One must perforce be uneasy, paradoxical, about reforms such as have been suggested in the foregoing chapters. They are modest enough, and enough within conventional bounds to be politically feasible; and this is a virtue in education, which suffers from the extremes of unexamined traditionalism and impolitic radicalism. Yet they are present-bound, and refer to current conditions, not to conditions that will prevail for those we are concerned with, the youngsters, in their adult lives. It is my hope that what I have proposed here looks both ways, that it has sufficient appeal to us today and to our current needs to be put into practice, and that it will have some clear relevance to the future. The demands of this future, however, go far beyond such remedies as shuffling institutions and fiddling with the mechanics of funding and examinations.

A common construction of the future is of technology rampant, of a culture of "things"—omnipresent television sets, instantly accessible computers, all kinds of sorting and classifying devices. The classroom-of-the-future seems to have been invented by Rube Goldberg; it looks like an advertisement for the ultimate automated kitchen. The technomania, as several critics have pointed out, is largely an illusion: the prohibitive expense of truly automatic teaching (particularly when it is computer-based) will see to that, as will the traditionalism of educators, who are uncomfortable when called upon to use new devices to teach old things. Technology in communication is likely to flourish much more in informal education. Cable television, which will greatly increase the number of channels available on a single set, satellites to extend the reach of a single signal, and recording devices that will allow individuals to copy programs and replay them or to own and play at will any program they have missed open possibilities of far greater variety in television than we have today. The technology of printing, already shaken by xerography, may sustain further shocks, such as the availability of inexpensive materials "printed" on demand by xerography right at an individual's console. These and other such developments will strikingly increase the variety and accessibility of vast quantities of information to the individual.

What the future holds (and, to a large extent, it's here already) is an *informal* educational system of immense power and variety. The culture will teach unremittingly, and with great effectiveness. Ours will be an information-rich culture of immense proportions; it is well on its way now. The information purveyed, however, will be largely unsystematic, unsustained, and not directed primarily to "teaching." Much of it will be structured to entertain first, and to inform second, if at all. It will greatly strengthen the hand of those who engage in mass persuasion, both in business and in politics.

The reaction of educators can take two forms. One would

be to "deschool," as Ivan Illich puts it (albeit in a somewhat different context).[1] Much vicarious learning comes informally in an information-rich culture, thus sharply reducing the need for schools to "teach about things"—current events, history, geography, descriptive science, rhetoric, and more. What is missing is experience and human contacts; these can be arranged for children quite informally, allowing youngsters to meet and work along with men and women of all schools of life, in factories, or laboratories, or hospitals, or homes. An information-rich culture, this argument goes, might properly call for an educational "system" resembling today's Trout Fishing in America more than a conventional school. Very likely, the informal media do a better job of teaching even now: can Mr. Chips or Miss Dove possibly compete with Walter Cronkite? A lot of school time is now wasted, being redundant with what the culture willy-nilly provides and will continue increasingly to provide. Eliminate formal schooling, then; but see that direct experience is provided for, as the necessary supplement to the vicarious and descriptive teaching supplied by video, print, and informal social contacts.

Such "deschooling" would, however, be a disaster. The presence of an impressing mass of information—unsystematic, persuasive, and inevitably both confusing and beguiling—puts a new kind of demand on an education system (whatever medium it chooses to use—classrooms, television transmission, books, or what not): the need for discrimination. American culture in the future promises to be an ever-growing cacophony of messages; the ability to sort these out, to understand, and to analyze them will be necessary for any significant kind of participation in the society. The illiterate barely makes it today; the gullible will be tomorrow's victim.

The school of the future (and, again, its form and technology are of secondary interest) must concentrate on

1. Ivan Illich, *Deschooling Society* (New York, 1970).

analysis, on intellectual discrimination, what has been heretofore called power. Perhaps the culture's increasingly rich communications will lessen the need for collegias to teach at agency, but the need to develop a child's ability to think perceptively will be ever greater. In this task, the schools (academies, in my construal) will be fundamentally countercyclical, devoted to preparing children to criticize and to resist the culture's vast communications system—and to see to its quality, balance, and variety as well. The schools should prepare people to be critics, not make them converts; in this sense, schools will be "revolutionary," and most constructively so. It remains to be seen whether Americans will be willing to support a system of schools (or academies) that really do teach intellectual discrimination, with all the criticism of the status quo that that implies. One cannot be sanguine in this thought; one can more easily foresee deschooling—which, at its worst, is a kind of romantic cop-out—than an increase in sophisticated and demanding intellectual training for all children.

Much is made in current futurist literature about the need for schools to teach adaptability—the ability to foresee, understand, and cope with social and technological change. Again, as in so many areas, one is forced back on the intellect, for qualities of perception and flexibility which support judgment are essential when an individual faces an unfamiliar situation. At the same time, one's ability to manage change—any new situation or surrounding—is undoubtedly a function of one's sense of agency; and society can, at least in part, help youngsters to gain such a sense. However, a culture rich in information—one that provides, in varied and sophisticated ways, an abundance of vicarious, "new" situations—may require even fewer formal collegia; at the same time it may require rigorous intellectual training for its children and adults. New situations (change) call for fresh analysis and the consideration of likely options (Given this new place and condition, what are the options I have and what are the most likely consequences of each, given the limited information available?). Such an assessment requires both a strong character and intellectual versatility. The second, relatively easier to teach than the first, is the right of every citizen.

Put another way, a culture that can purvey masses of information effectively can, more easily than ever before in history, control the minds of its citizens. The only defense against a dull cultural homogeneity (or worse) is an educational system that helps individuals to become critical and resistant to unwanted persuasion by powerful media. This end cannot be reached by institutional juggling—by creating this kind of school, rather than that—for what is here required is more discriminating *individuals.* Corporately these individuals (it is bravely hypothesized) will be wiser and more humane in their social policies than we have been. If we cannot believe as much, why have education at all?

A consequence of the rapid technological advance in communications is the narrowing of distances on the globe, narrowing in several senses. Air travel has brought people closer together in time, though only a tiny fraction of mankind—but an influential fraction—is directly affected. On a mass scale, inexpensive transistor radios carry voices over thousands of miles: many peoples are hearing at first hand ideas up to now foreign to them. Inexpensive television sets will be readily available in a few decades. While the wealthy Western nations are engulfed in a "richness" of information, even the least economically favored countries in the world will be receiving signals from other quarters and other cultures. We will become even more so what has accurately been termed a "global village."

But the interrelatedness of nations and peoples goes beyond probable increases in communications. National boundaries have less and less meaning in economic life, as the beginnings of regional "markets" testify. Every rich nation is working to develop substitutes for raw materials now imported from other countries; but the fact remains that most economies, even the wealthiest, depend on the resources and trade of others. The vast, multinational corporations (whether private, as in the West, or public as in the Communist world) are testimony to that, and they will increase in number and influence, as will the international labor movement.

Issues of national security profoundly and obviously link countries. And when the territory, economic wealth, and employment of a people are affected, governments act. A network of formal and informal interconnections among nations has developed since the end of World War II. As Zbigniew Brzezinski writes:

> The world is ceasing to be an arena in which relatively self-contained, "sovereign," and homogeneous nations intersect, collaborate, clash or make war . . . Weapons of total destructive power can be applied at any point on the globe in a matter of minutes—in less time, in fact, than it takes for police in a major city to respond to an emergency call. The entire globe is in closer reach and touch than a middle-sized European power was to its own capital fifty years ago. Transnational ties are gaining in importance, while the claims of nationalism, though still intense, are nonetheless becoming diluted.[2]

However, Brzezinski observes, the "real unity of mankind remains remote"; and therein lies the fundamental fact about our future. Curiously, many American "futurologists," particularly those writing about education, completely ignore this reality. They myopically foresee an altogether chauvinist future, one that assumes ever greater American wealth unruffled by international passions or demands. The predicted

2. Zbigniew Brzezinski, *Between Two Ages: America's Role in the Technetronic Era* (New York, 1970), pp. 3, 4, 5.

technomania would not be the outlandish vision it so often is if America could develop autonomously. Of course, it does not now, and cannot.

Seen from an educational vantage point, many of America's current internal problems have international counterparts of frightening dimensions. The inequalities of America seem trivial when set against worldwide reality: the rich nations are very rich, and the poor very poor, and the distance between is widening. We consider how the poor in America can be helped to break out of their cycle of poverty: how can one break a far more persistent cycle in, say, Bengal or Chad? We talk of educating autonomous people who wisely balance individual ends with larger social goals and who can accommodate themselves to a general concept of justice: do these things have any relevance today for a South African black or the denizen of a Rio de Janiero *favella*? America professes to be fighting a war on poverty, with several billions of dollars a year: What financial effort would be required from the rich nations to bring poor people internationally to a standard of living comparable to even the worst found in the United States? The questions are, of course, both germane and absurd. One cannot begin to approach issues of human equality and individual dignity on an international scale from the same aspect or in the same terms as used for the United States alone; but it still remains true that all human beings deserve comparable dignity and rights.

Worldwide individual human rights *are* an American concern, for two reasons. First, it is elementary justice that those who have should help those who have not. If America wants a soul for itself, it cannot flinch from its monumental international moral obligation, an obligation for which it will have to sacrifice. Second, a selfish America would shrivel, as the Third World slowly gains power and autonomy. The days of weak nations abjectly providing raw materials (and thus capital) and markets (and still further profits) to the stronger are passing. The signs are unmistakable: even someone so traditionally friendly to the West as the Shah of Iran is now driving hard bargains with Western oil companies; two decades ago, this would have been unthinkable. The Third World is becoming cheeky, arrogant, prideful—quite like the American black. Colonial and neocolonial days are speeding to an end, and the West must adjust to that economic and political reality. Indeed, the West must applaud it, for the very arrogance that the rich nations find so galling is evidence of the self-assurance upon which autonomous peoples can build for themselves.

That the racial issue is more pronounced internationally than domestically is self-evident; indeed, the position of the races is reversed. Whereas in America the dominating race is also the most numerous, on a worldwide scale those with yellow, brown, and black skins are the least wealthy but in the greatest numbers. A quarter of mankind is Chinese—four Chinese for every American—and the proportion is rising: most Americans simply fail to understand and appreciate this fact. There are many more Indians who are as poor or poorer than the poorest United States citizen than there are Americans at every level of wealth. Yet Americans continue to patronize non-Western cultures and to dismiss all nonwhite peoples as rather curious "wogs." Equally disastrous is the myopia of American liberals, mesmerized as they seem to be with domestic concerns: they constitute the group that one might expect to lead in an internationalist attitude and in a critique of American international racism. And the most isolationist and chauvinist of all may be America's so-called radicals, small though that group is.

The "colored" peoples (of course, pink is a color, and that is what Caucasians are) do not require American good wishes to find their self-respect, as Mao Tse-tung has amply demonstrated. But it is indisputably better for Americans, and for world stability—not to say happiness (a factor that is never part of the rhetoric of high diplomacy)—that Americans find a just accommodation with the fact that they are people of the world and only secondarily of a country and that their immense wealth and good fortune obligate them to help those who are less fortunate. This does not mean that they should become Lady Bountiful, distributing largesse to the grateful poor: the process of wise aid is far more complex than that. And, to boot, the inherent "right" of Western peoples to most of the usable wealth on the planet is highly questionable. That, by and large, the whites are the haves and the nonwhites the have-nots immeasurably complicates the problem. Race war, in a variety of forms, is an ever-present threat.

The problems of justice and order are complex enough in the United States, but infinitely more so on a global scale. An information-rich society with a broadly established culture has the luxury of shared beliefs about human and property rights. There are strains on these beliefs, inevitably, but these are manageable, given political will. Internationally, there is no central agency for the exercise of global "political will." Muddying the issue is the fact that there are few widely shared beliefs about human justice, and even when there seems to be some agreement, there isn't a common way of enforcing it. Different cultures "see" relationships in differing ways, inevitably alien to each other; and while this diversity is enriching, it complicates the establishment of any kind of global equilibrium or order. Differences in perception and belief are obvious in such areas as population growth; but they are subtler, more complex, and less understood in other areas, as in the concept of the role and obligations of the family. Language is a vehicle of thought; and the differences in language reflect profound differences in world views. Some are broadening, if simple: in some languages, colors are verbs; in others (such as ours), they are adjectives. How different a tree seems when it greens!—one's view and understanding of color take on new dimensions. Some differences are more troublesome, as in the concepts of inclusion and exclusion:

some languages provide sharp delineations ("all," "none"); some not so sharp, emphasizing in daily speech the shades of gray, the special, individual character of every action. There are many other examples: but the point is not to make an argument for language reform but rather to point up language differences as manifestations of important differences among peoples' views. The same things and concepts seem different to individuals from contrasting cultures. The problem of world order and peace is monumentally more complicated because of this.

What can the developed West do? Share its wealth in generous and sensitive measure (a topic of immense importance and quite beyond the scope of this book). Provide know-how or, as the trade calls it, technical assistance, and relevant research. The formally educated West has knowledge that the poorer nations can use; moreover, it has knowledge of how to create new, usable knowledge. Such information and skills, it must be understood, may eventually be turned against the West. (Europeans never realized that Egyptians, if trained, could in fact operate the Suez Canal; they learned better after 1956.) Such knowledge will increase a region's self-possession and power and will decrease its dependence on the richer nations. Most important, the West must change its own attitudes, must create among its own people the will to alter conditions of inequality and misery both at home and abroad, must lessen the psychological hold of localism and nationalism on its own people. As Gunnar Myrdal has asserted, "The primordial problem is, therefore, *how people in the developed countries think and feel about helping underdeveloped countries* in their development efforts."[3]

Structural reforms—such as creating the United Nations— are meaningless unless there is political belief behind them, conviction that these new structures should have power.

3. Gunnar Myrdal, *The Challenge of World Poverty: A World Anti-Poverty Program in Outline* (New York, 1970), p. 310 (italics in the original).

Again, this requires that the rich nations—the United States among them—perceive their role and obligations in new ways. To quote Myrdal again: what is needed is "an intellectual and moral catharsis."[4] Given his perceptive prediction in the 1940's of the American racial predicament, his current warnings of and remedies for international crisis must be taken seriously. What is needed is a shift of opinion among the populace, a shift in public attitude, a new sympathy for the human condition and a commitment to improving it. This is where education plays its part.

From the educator's point of view, then, the two central forces of future change are increased information and communication, and global interrelatedness. Neither condition is addressed well by structural reform. Both require an overall reaction among the people, a change in the attitudes of the millions. Such a prospect seems hopeless at first glance, particularly so to those who traditionally construe economic and social development in aggregate terms. But the fact remains that no shortcut, no levering of markets or imposition of new governmental forms, will have much impact if it is not accompanied by public support. A single example will suffice: land reform in India and Pakistan, while legislatively mandatory and a part of nationalist rhetoric since independence, has made no headway. It simply has not taken place. Why? Because upper-class people do not want to reduce their incomes and status, and the landless poor are apathetic and disorganized. The attitudes of both need to be changed, or misery of one kind or another will exist forever. Laws do not help if the mass of people do not want to act upon them. Lest Americans feel smug at this point, let them reread the Constitution and reflect on how well we have carried out those dicta of American justice.

Our policy problem in a large degree stems from the

4. Ibid., p. xii.

manner in which we construe our task. American policy, as was indicated in chapter one, puts a relatively low probability on the likelihood that education will successfully alter American attitudes. Progressive thought in the seventies implicitly assumes that schools (of any kind) do not "work," and that indirect manipulation of the structure of society is the only way. American critics and policy makers are markedly determinist about popular opinion and cast a patronizing but suspicious eye both on those who suggest that education *can* make a difference if it is handled effectively and on those who hold that education represents the only real solution to many public problems such as bigotry.

Furthermore, we are mesmerized by a conception of *development* that is primarily economic. We focus on the measurable "things" of a society—the number of schools and their pupils, the extent of the communications system (the "infrastructure," the moguls call it), the balance of international payments. There is no misery quotient, no place for pride (even when the presence of misery and the absence of pride may be the prime causes of sluggish economic development). Again, one must look at the Negro's rise in the United States: until there was popular indignation (largely among blacks themselves) at the continued misery in the midst of American affluence, and until group pride was fostered, there was little progress. Americans are paralyzed by what the English Kenneth Clark has aptly called "heroic materialism": a glory in the size of measurable things. The American view of the worth of growth follows upon this.

Of course, development is only one way to conceive of a satisfying culture. Another might be equilibrium: a just but stable society, its merit partially stemming from its limited growth (the Scandinavian countries and Switzerland suggest the usefulness of this construal). A joyful society or even a just society—even if these mean less material growth (a prospect difficult for Americans to comprehend)—are now conceptions appealing only to the extremist utopian, the

Gauguin who exalts a (supposedly) bucolic and happy Tahiti. But the concept of a just and joyful culture deserves better than the distortions of myopic romantics; it is a measure of American timidity and shortsightedness that it has not gone beyond that. Most American liberals are even embarrassed to think along these lines.

Social reform—even reform of limited scope, as outlined in the preceding chapters—*requires* popular will, requires the aggregated opinion of individuals determined to change priorities and opinions. The reforms that are desperately needed are reforms *primarily* attained through altered public opinion; they are not issues that can be managed within existing conventional wisdom. The problems are bigger and the solutions inevitably too revolutionary for that. This condition can lead to despair and a host of determinist self-fulfilling prophesies and debilitating predictions of doom. Or it can lead to a rediscovery of education as a vehicle for public action and a commitment to use it wisely for reform. Education is dangerous, of course: it can be used to distort and enslave. At its best, it is revolutionary: fostering people's ability to examine their surroundings clearly and accurately leads to some nasty discoveries. But, volatile though it is, education remains the best hope of a free people.

Fortunately, the process of political change itself educates. If an awareness of future reality dawns on some of the public, and if the country can once again spawn a group of hopeful, if also practical, leaders, an ennobling process of education and reeducation of individuals can emerge, fostered by the very technologies which now seem to narrow and constrict us.

Acknowledgments
and Sources

Acknowledgments
and Sources

A book of speculations such as this one is one side of a conversation, questions phrased in the form of assertions. For years the other protagonist, my principal intellectual colleague, has been Nancy Faust Sizer, who also happens to be my wife. As a scholar of Asia, she has brought skepticism to my chauvinism. As a teacher in a city high school, she urged me continually to see the world as it is, satisfied, sometimes apathetic, sometimes anguished, but hopeful yet. As a partner on long rambles on the moors of Somerset, she reminded me that these speculations are but one cut at the issue of reform, and not necessarily the best one at that; her reservations were gently, but firmly made. Our children, Tod, Judy, Hal, and Lyde thoughtfully tolerated our conversations with good humor and whimsical acceptance. I am grateful. Of such sharing are intensely rewarding partnerships made.

I have other debts, most notably to Lawrence A. Cremin, whose persistent encouragement to a wide circle of colleagues provokes the best in many of us. Cremin's "invisible college" of historians and erstwhile historians has had a profound effect on the university study of education. To my dozens of friends at Harvard I have similar obligations; they have remained optimistic and supportive during difficult times. The endless talk and study in Longfellow and Larsen Halls at Harvard has shaped my ideas fundamentally. Donald Oliver's

163

abrasive skepticism has been always helpful. His "Education and Community" (coauthored with Fred Newmann and first appearing in the *Harvard Educational Review*, Winter 1967) exemplifies how his thoughts have influenced mine. Adam Curle's notion of "awareness," which he has fully outlined in his new book, *Militants and Mystics* (Tavistock: London, 1972), goes well beyond my notions of "agency." Adam's persistent humanity has been a great influence. John Shlien, Gerald Lesser, and Lawrence Kohlberg all read my manuscript. I am especially indebted to the first for urging me to be less apologetic for my liberalism. John's own notions of the need to "promote the process of invention" within far more equalitarian (or "public") settings have been very influential, as have Gerry's and Larry's approaches of relating understanding of human development to practical approaches in society to help children. The debts to others are also great: one learns much—often in spite of oneself—in any learning community as lively as the School of Education as been.

Thanks are due the John Simon Guggenheim Foundation for providing support for a brief leave in England during the spring and summer of 1971 and the University of Bristol, especially Ben and Margaret Morris there, for welcoming me to that company. A special debt is owed Dana M. Cotton, who agreed to shoulder my duties as Acting Dean and who protected the privacy of my months abroad with exemplary charity.

I am indebted to Ann Orlov and Mark Carroll for encouraging me with my work and bringing it to publication. And thanks are due Felicity Wilson-Rudd and Mary Williams Mellon for preparing the manuscript.

I have drawn ideas from many secondary works. The following is a list of books mentioned or alluded to in the text, or which I otherwise found directly useful.

Ashton-Warner, Sylvia. *Teacher*. New York: Simon and Schuster, 1963.
Bailyn, Bernard. *Education in the Forming of American Society*. Chapel Hill: University of North Carolina Press, 1960.

Banfield, Edward C. *The Unheavenly City: The Nature and Future of Our Urban Crisis.* Boston: Little, Brown, 1970.

Bestor, Arthur. *Educational Wastelands.* Urbana: University of Illinois Press, 1953.

Bloom, Benjamin. *A Taxonomy of Educational Objectives.* New York: D. McKay, 1961.

Boulding, Kenneth. *The Meaning of the Twentieth Century: The Great Transition.* New York: Harper and Row, 1964.

Brown, Claude. *Manchild in the Promised Land.* New York: New American Library, 1965.

Bruner, Jerome. *On Knowing: Essays for the Left Hand.* Cambridge: Harvard University Press, 1962.

The Process of Education. Cambridge: Harvard University Press, 1960.

Brzezinski, Zbigniew. *Between Two Ages: America's Role in the Technetronic Era.* New York: Viking, 1970.

Clark, Kenneth B. *Dark Ghetto: Dilemmas of Social Power.* New York: Harper and Row, 1965.

A Design for the Attainment of High Academic Achievement for the Students of the Public Elementary and Junior High Schools of Washington, D.C. New York: Metropolitan Applied Research Council, 1970.

Coleman, James, et al. *Equality of Educational Opportunity.* Washington, D.C.: Government Printing Office, 1966.

Coleman, James S., ed. *Education and Political Development.* Princeton: Princeton University Press, 1965.

Conant, James B. *The American High School Today.* New York: McGraw-Hill, 1959.

Slums and Suburbs. New York: McGraw-Hill, 1961.

Cremin, Lawrence A. *The American Common School: An Historic Conception.* New York: Teachers College Press, 1951.

American Education: The Colonial Experience. New York: Harper and Row, 1970.

The Genius of American Education. Pittsburgh: University of Pittsburgh Press, 1965.

The Transformation of the School. New York: Knopf, 1961.

Dennison, George. *The Lives of Children: The Story of the First Street School.* New York: Random House, 1969.

Dewey, John. *Democracy and Education.* New York: Macmillan, 1916.

Drucker, Peter F. *The Age of Discontinuity: Guidelines to Our Changing Society.* New York: Harper and Row, 1969.

Featherstone, Joseph. *Schools Where Children Learn.* New York: Liveright, 1971.

Flesch, Rudolph. *Why Johnny Can't Read.* New York: Harper and Row, 1955.

Friedenburg, Edgar Z. *Coming of Age in America: Growth and Acquiescence.* New York: Random House, 1965.

Galbraith, John Kenneth. *The New Industrial State.* Boston: Houghton Mifflin, 1967.

Glazer, Nathan, and Moynihan, Daniel P. *Beyond the Melting Pot.* 2d ed. Cambridge: M.I.T. Press, 1970.

Goodman, Paul. *Compulsory Mis-Education.* New York: Vintage, 1966. *Growing Up Absurd.* New York: Random House, 1960.

Grant, Nigel. *Soviet Education.* Hammondsworth [U.K.]: Penguin, 1964.

Hacker, Andrew. *The End of the American Era.* New York: Atheneum, 1970.

Harbison, Frederick H., and Myers, Charles A. *Education, Manpower, and Economic Growth: Strategies of Human Resource Development.* New York: McGraw-Hill, 1964.

Harrington, Michael. *Toward a Democratic Left.* New York: Macmillan, 1968.

Haskins, Jim. *Diary of a Harlem Schoolteacher.* New York: Grove Press, 1969.

Hentoff, Nat. *Our Children Are Dying.* New York: Viking, 1967.

Herndon, James. *The Way It Spozed To Be.* New York: Simon and Schuster, 1968.

Holt, John. *How Children Fail.* New York: Pitman, 1964.

Katz, Michael B. *The Irony of Early School Reform.* Cambridge: Harvard University Press, 1968.
Class, Bureaucracy, and Schools. New York: Praeger, 1971.

Kaufman, Bel. *Up the Down Staircase.* Englewood Cliffs: Prentice-Hall, 1965.

Keppel, Francis. *Personnel Policies for Public Education.* Pittsburgh: University of Pittsburgh Press, 1961.

Koerner, James B. *The Case for Basic Education.* Boston: Little, Brown, 1959.

Kohl, Herbert R. *Thirty-Six Children.* New York: New America Library, 1967.

Kohlberg, Lawrence. "Education for Justice: A Modern Statement of the Platonic View." In *Moral Education: Five Lectures.* Cambridge: Harvard University Press, 1970.

Kozol, Jonathan. *Death at an Early Age.* Boston: Houghton Mifflin, 1967.

Latimer, John T. *What's Happened to Our High Schools?* Washington, D.C.: Public Affairs Press, 1958.

Leonard, George B. *Education and Ecstasy.* New York: Delacorte, 1968.

Lynd, Albert. *Quackery in the Public Schools.* Boston: Little, Brown, 1953.

Machlup, Fritz. *The Production and Distribution of Knowledge in the United States.* Princeton: Princeton University Press, 1962.

Martin W.T., and Pinck, Dan C., eds. *Curriculum Improvement and*

Innovation: A Partnership of Students, School Teachers, and Research Scholars. Cambridge, Mass.: R. Bentley, 1966.

Mayer, Martin. *The Schools.* New York: Harper and Row, 1961.

Myrdal, Gunnar. *An American Dilemma.* New York: Harper and Row, 1944.

The Challenge of World Poverty: A World Anti-Poverty Program in Outline. New York: Pantheon, 1970.

Oettinger, Anthony G., with Marks, Sema. *Run, Computer, Run.* Cambridge: Harvard University Press, 1969.

Packard, Vance. *The Hidden Persuaders.* New York: McKay, 1957.

Postman, Neil, and Weingartner, Charles. *Teaching as a Subversive Activity.* New York: Delacorte, 1969.

Reich, Charles A. *The Greening of America.* New York: Random House, 1970.

Rickover, Hyman, *Education and Freedom.* New York: Dutton, 1959. "Education for All Children: What We Can Learn from England." Washington, D.C.: Government Printing Office, 1962.

Rosenthal, Robert, and Jacobsen, Lenore. *Pygmalion in the Classroom.* New York: Holt, Rinehart, and Winston, 1968.

Scheffler, Israel. "Philosophical Models of Teaching," *Harvard Educational Review* vol. 33, no. 2 (Spring 1965), pp. 131-143.

Silberman, Charles. *Crisis in the Classroom.* New York: Random House, 1970.

Sizer, Theodore R. *The Age of the Academies.* New York: Teachers College Press, 1964.

Secondary Schools at the Turn of the Century. New Haven: Yale University Press, 1964.

Skidelsky, Robert. *English Progressive Schools.* Hammondsworth [U.K.] : Penguin, 1969.

Skinner, Burrhus Frederic. *The Technology of Teaching.* New York: Appleton-Century-Crofts, 1968.

Stodolsky, Susan, and Lesser, Gerald S. "Learning Patterns in the Disadvantaged." *Harvard Educational Review* vol. 37, no. 4 (Fall 1967), pp. 546-593.

Toffler, Alvin. *Future Shock.* New York: Random House, 1970.

Whitehead, Alfred North. *The Aims of Education.* New York: Macmillan, 1929.